Public Debt in Kenya

Public debt in developing economies has increased dramatically over the last 20 years, with debt repayment obligations putting the livelihoods of millions of individuals at risk and threatening to stall progress toward lowering poverty rates and achieving long-term development objectives across many countries, especially in sub-Saharan Africa. Debt fragility is a systemic issue that affects many countries spanning different continents, regardless of the idiosyncratic nature of each country's system of government and drivers of growth. Kenya is one of these fragile economies, currently classified as an economy at high risk of default.

This book gives a historical economic account of public debt in Kenya, dating back to the late 1800s. It describes the key episodes and events that resulted in the accumulation of debt and gives an intuitive understanding of the economic dynamics of debt during the precolonial, colonial, and postcolonial periods in Kenya's history. Existing studies on Kenya's public debt are either not comprehensive, choosing to focus on a narrow period, or are technical empirical analyses, rendering them inaccessible to a large audience. By describing the dynamics of public debt in Kenya, the book increases familiarity with a topic that has important implications for Kenya, and which has occupied a central stage in Kenya's policy debates in the recent past.

History shows that contagion from economic crises is not unique and isolated to individual nations, thus the book is relevant not only for policy debates in Kenya, but also for other low-income and emerging economies within sub-Saharan Africa.

Aaron Thegeya is an economist who obtained his Ph.D. in economics from the University of Oxford as a Rhodes Scholar. He was Senior Economic Advisor to the Deputy Chief of Staff, Executive Office of the President of Kenya, and has worked as an economist at the International Monetary Fund and the World Bank.

Routledge Studies in Development Economics

201. Financial Inclusion and Sustainable Development in Sub-Saharan Africa
Edited by David Mhlanga and Mufaro Dzingirai

202. Natural Capital and Climate Smart Agriculture
Measuring Progress towards Sustainability and Policy Making in India
Pradyot Ranjan Jena, Shunsuke Managi and Ritanjali Majhi

203. Project Finance in Africa
Principles and Applications
Joshua Yindenaba Abor, Elikplimi Komla Agbloyor, Paul Gbahabo, Saint Kuttu, Ashenafi Fanta and Baah Aye Kusi

204. Debt Crises and Sovereign Risk in Africa
Ndzalama Mathebula

205. Artificial Intelligence and SMEs in Developing Economies
Edited by Timilehin Olasoji Olubiyi and Tulus T.H. Tambunan

206. Public Debt in Kenya
An Economic History
Aaron Thegeya

For more information about this series, please visit: www.routledge.com/Routledge-Studies-in-Development-Economics/book-series/SE0266

Public Debt in Kenya

An Economic History

Aaron Thegeya

Routledge
Taylor & Francis Group
LONDON AND NEW YORK

First published 2026
by Routledge
4 Park Square, Milton Park, Abingdon, Oxon OX14 4RN

and by Routledge
605 Third Avenue, New York, NY 10158

Routledge is an imprint of the Taylor & Francis Group, an informa business

British Library Cataloguing-in-Publication Data
A catalogue record for this book is available from the British Library

ISBN: 978-1-041-09164-6 (hbk)
ISBN: 978-1-041-09179-0 (pbk)
ISBN: 978-1-003-64882-6 (ebk)

DOI: 10.4324/9781003648826

Typeset in Times New Roman
by Newgen Publishing UK

Contents

Preface

Despite the enormous costs that economic crises impose on countries, the global economy is surprisingly incapable of maintaining uninterrupted and sustained growth. Each period of economic expansion is invariably disrupted by a painful contraction that causes widespread hardship, affecting particularly vulnerable individuals with low savings the most. Also puzzling is that although each crisis is distinct in terms of its immediate trigger, there is a major overlap in terms of the characteristics that crises which have occurred over history share. One of the frequently recurrent features is a build-up of debt to a point of unsustainability, whereby the sudden unwinding of liabilities, or inability to roll over payments that are due, triggers a default event. A large economic literature has studied the role that debt has played in global economic development, and continues to do. However, there is no birds-eye study of the role that debt has played in Kenya's economic development. This book intends to fill this gap.

This book is written as an accessible economic history of public debt in Kenya. The intended audience is any person with an interest and basic knowledge, but without a technical background in economics. Therefore, the focus of the book is, first and foremost, on giving a historical account of the key episodes and events in Kenya's history that influenced the accumulation as well as the repayment of public debt, dating back to the late 1800s. And second, the book gives an intuitive understanding of the economic dynamics influencing public debt. The scope of the book is restricted to public debt, which is debt accumulated and owed by a sovereign nation, rather than private debt, which is accumulated by either firms or households.

However, the book goes beyond a macroeconomic analysis to give political economy insights.

The motivation behind the book is that existing studies are either not comprehensive, choosing to focus on a narrow period, or are empirical analyses which by their technical nature are inaccessible to a large audience. By describing the dynamics of debt in Kenya, the book aims to increase broad familiarity among both economists and non-economists with a topic that has important implications for Kenya. The book attempts to draw broad lessons on the basis of the historical timeline of debt by examining public policy documents as well as the wealth of academic literature on debt. However, the book is not an empirical analysis in its own right.

The book relies on a wealth of information from different resources, including Article IV reports, which are regular surveillance reports published by the International Monetary Fund (IMF) on the macroeconomic status of economies, including archived declassified reports. Additionally, Kenyan development plans, data from economic surveys and other statistical archives, academic research publications and policy documents from various institutions are relied upon to construct the timeline of events.

Acknowledgments

I gratefully acknowledge support from Financial Sector Deepening Kenya (FSD Kenya). I thank Julius Muia, David Ndii, Kenneth Njendu and Justin Willis for their reviews and helpful comments. I am grateful to Safiatu Diallo and Amrik Heyer for their discussions and insights.

Introduction

Africa is a continent abundant in natural resources. The resource endowment of the Democratic Republic of Congo alone has the potential to feed over 2 billion people, more than the entire population of Africa, given its favorable climate and abundance of fertile soil.[1] And yet Africa as a continent is today a net importer of agricultural produce, with resource-rich and fragile economies in particular responsible for the agricultural trade deficit.[2] With its growing young population and rapid urbanization, Africa has been conceptualized as the "last frontier" of development in the global economy, with massive potential to realize a demographic dividend by utilizing the skills of its growing labor force as its young population increasingly enters the workforce in order to accelerate economic growth and improve living standards for all. However, on the anniversary of 60 years of independence for most African economies, employment remains a major challenge, and economies are supported—by default—by a vibrant informal sector that absorbs the majority of the labor force.

Some serious questions are raised about why African economies have struggled to grow. Comparisons are frequently made between major African economies and the Asian Tigers[3] to draw out possible explanations for this low-growth trajectory puzzle. Excluding countries embroiled in conflict, even relatively stable economies that took off strongly following independence eventually lost momentum. Kenya, for a while lauded globally as the shining African model of how to develop a post-colonial economy, grew at an average rate of 7 percent in the 1960s, before its growth trajectory eventually tailed off by the end of the 1970s. In particular, the divergence in growth paths between Kenya and the Republic of Korea offers a lucid

DOI: 10.4324/9781003648826-1

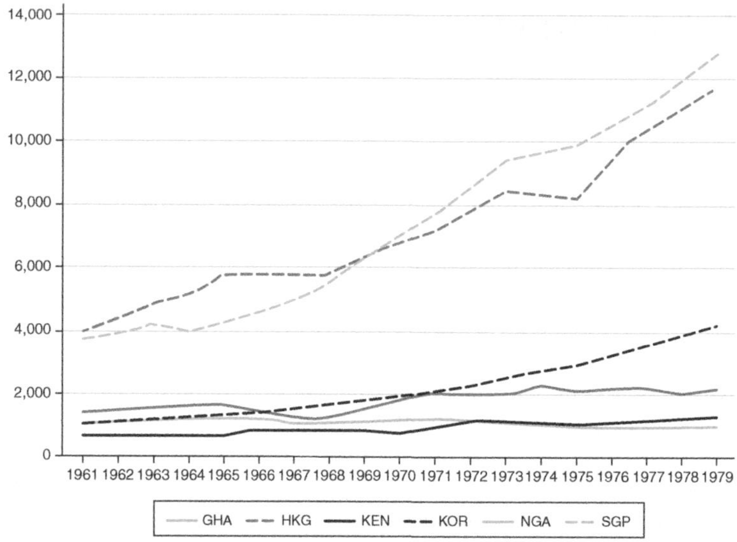

Figure 0.1 GDP per capita in select African and Asian economies (percent, constant 2015 US$).

Source: Data from World Bank World Development Indicators database.

example. Korea's income per capita increased from a level similar to Kenya's in 1960 to 3.4 times by 1979, and the gap widened further to a factor of 19 times by 2022. Kenya is not alone. Ghana and Nigeria, which gained independence prior to Kenya, have not fared much better. In particular, despite the boost provided by its booming oil exports during the 1960s and 1970s, Nigeria's living standards did not see much improvement by 1979 (Figure 0.1).

A major and well-understood barrier to the development of newly independent African economies, to which Kenya was no exception, was the low level of domestic savings, which is the difference between total national income and final consumption expenditure. A country with high savings is naturally more capable of higher levels of productivity-enhancing domestic investment to boost growth. However, although Kenya had low domestic savings in the 1960s, Korea had even lower levels due in particular to higher household consumption, even though government consumption was lower in comparison to Kenya. Specifically, Kenya's domestic savings rate in the 1960s was on average 18 percent in comparison to 11 percent in Korea. Despite similarly poor domestic conditions, Korea was able to experience an economic transformation "miracle" to become a global economic powerhouse while Kenya lagged behind. Korea's domestic savings rate increased rapidly to 38 percent by the 1990s and thereafter remained at a level above 30 percent. In contrast, Kenya's domestic savings rate stagnated at about 20 percent until the end of the 1980s, when it thereafter fell precipitously to less than half its value at independence by the turn of the century. Contributing to the divergence of paths was the greater ability of Korea to leverage public savings as well as increase the household savings rate, while Kenyan households decreased their savings rate.

Evidently, despite Kenya's valiant efforts and significant progress in improving living standards during the first decade following independence, the economy was already on a lower growth trajectory than Asian peer economies. Were structural factors already at play, and did Kenya's development as a newly independent country with high aspirations begin with a serious handicap? Kenya's identity as an African Socialist economy was clearly articulated and ambitious, recognizing the major development initiatives that required implementation and identifying the obstacles that needed to be overcome to achieve economic transformation. The nascent government institutions at that point in time were not inhibited by poor governance concerns. Despite this foundation, the inability of the economy to achieve sustained growth in spite of the best efforts exerted by the administration remains a puzzle.

Development is complex and multifaceted. In fact, social scientists frequently disagree on what development itself means, and contributions by professionals across different fields have drawn attention to a large collection of factors that contribute both to the meaning and determinants of development. Among the many dimensions included are improvements in the well-being of individuals, especially across income, education completion rates and health outcomes as measured by indicators such as life expectancy or childhood mortality rates. Other important factors are the sustainability and permanence of such improvements as well as the distribution of growth, as measured by levels of inequality. Fortunate or not, one may convincingly argue that economists have tended to dominate the dialogue on development. Traditionally, economists have focused on a narrow definition of development that tracks the average increase in income per capita, under the premise that other indicators of welfare improvement are likely to be positively correlated with income. While this narrow focus has undoubtedly contributed to a tangible basis for tracking development over time that is comparable across countries, it has also placed lower emphasis on some critical dimensions of development from a holistic perspective, many of which have deteriorated over time. Despite continued efforts today to track the multi-dimensional aspects of development better, one may argue that the focus on income continues to play the most central role.

This book is written from an economist's perspective and focuses on the role that debt has played in influencing development in Kenya. The analysis abstracts from other factors but also draws relevant links to some influential dynamics, including the political environment. While the analysis is idiosyncratic to the case of Kenya, it bears keeping in mind that despite the heterogenous paths that other African economies have taken to develop and despite the major disparities in their endowments of natural resources, overall growth outcomes across sub-Saharan Africa have uniformly been significantly lower than any other region of the world.

Debt is a contract that transfers an asset from one party to another and simultaneously creates an obligation for the party that received the asset to make a payment at some point in the future. There are many good reasons to incur debt, the most obvious of which is to benefit from one's future potential today. Debt can play a decisive role in determining whether a person's potential is actually realized by paying upfront for important factors that build human capital, such as education and health care. The human capital paid for and developed by debt in turn improves the person's productivity and—hopefully—standards of living, thereby enabling the person to pay back the borrowed funds. This concept is applicable both from a household and national perspective. Countries with young populations, growing pools of productive labor potential and low stocks of human and physical capital also have lower rates of old-age dependency and obligations to provide social benefits to the elderly. Such economies frequently borrow to finance improvements in human capital as well as to improve physical infrastructure that supports higher productivity. These investments generate higher economic returns that finance the repayment of debt and create wealth through social security contributions, which in the future are used to pay for increasing dependency as the labor force ages. From this perspective, the origination of debt to support development may be termed not only as desirable but also perhaps even essential.

However, debt contracts create future obligations on borrowing parties that give rise to power dynamics. Debt contracted by a country imposes a burden of repayment on every living citizen and on the country's future generations with the likelihood of higher taxes, even though in practice debt contracts are agreed upon by a few elected representatives on behalf of the country. Failure to deliver on the objectives for which debt is contracted poses a massive risk, particularly in the case where misappropriation of funds and poor governance lead to deficient project implementation or project failure and in turn create an unequal distribution of liabilities and benefits, with large returns secured by a small political elite but the burden of repayment left to the broader population. In such cases, the social contract between citizens and their elected representatives is broken, and institutional failure prevails. At an individual level these dynamics give rise to a deep sense of social injustice. From this perspective, debt is a highly emotive subject. The influence of external parties may exacerbate these dynamics even further. When the major share of public debt is owed to external parties, the sense of accountability to the local population is further diminished; after all, public office is answerable to foreign individuals and not its domestic constituents. The external parties also leverage debt contracts to pursue their own interests, which may not align with the best course for the economy.

In this book we explore four key aspects of debt in the context of Kenya. The first, and most important, is the use of debt to stimulate long-term economic growth by virtue of increasing productivity. This occurs by deploying borrowed funds to invest in human and physical capital, thus increasing the ability of the working-age population to be productive through investment in education and healthcare and building enabling infrastructure such as roads to connect marketplaces or providing universal access to electricity to firms and households. The intention is that by virtue of those improvements, the economy can be put on a higher growth trajectory that then enables it to repay its debt while enjoying an increase in living standards.

The second aspect relates to the use of debt to respond to short-term shocks. This is closely related to the vulnerability of the economy to domestic and external shocks, such as erratic weather patterns or volatility in prices of key import commodities, such as fuel. The use of debt in these situations allows the economy to overcome the high and sudden expenditure needs that arise as a consequence of shocks and, critically, provides funds to support the livelihoods of vulnerable individuals that are most adversely impacted by the shocks. Additionally, in the event that shocks lower domestic demand below the potential of the economy, debt can serve as a stimulus to boost demand over the short term, and therefore serve as a buffer to lower the severity of the shocks' impact on economic performance.

Third, we explore the impact of debt on incentives, due to the fact that contracting parties rarely have perfect information about each other. Imperfect information influences the behavior of the parties and may result in suboptimal outcomes due to two types of problems: adverse selection, which refers to the inability to assess accurately the quality of the counterparty or the terms of the contract, or moral hazard, which refers to the inability to ensure that the counterparty exerts the level of effort required to honor the terms of the contract. These issues influence the global financial architecture and affect critical aspects of debt, including how much debt is taken on, the incentives to default on existing debt and the terms of negotiation in case of debt distress.

And finally, we explore the use of debt as a tool to promote ideologies, a topic that is within the realm of political economy. The need to borrow, coupled with the limited availability of sources of debt financing, allows originators of debt to attach conditions to the availability of debt in order to further their own interests, which may or may not align with what is best for the domestic economy. Additionally, governance and accountability in fulfilling the social contract between elected officials and citizens are a central aspect of political economy, where corrupt individuals may use public funds to their own benefit, knowing that the liability of repayment lies with all citizens.

We observe a number of persistent storylines that we explore in detail within the subsequent chapters. A fundamental observation is that despite the accumulation of debt over its history, Kenya has failed to live up to its growth potential. This is evidenced by the fact that Kenya has consistently failed to meet its growth targets as specified in detailed economic development plans and also evidenced by the widening gap between Kenya's per-capita growth since the 1960s relative to that of East-Asian economies, some of which were at a similar level of per-capita income at that point in time but which subsequently experienced rapid and sustained growth. Thus, although economies in other parts of the world have managed to converge more quickly to the income levels of more industrialized nations, Kenya has seen a lower growth trajectory, which has admittedly led to improved living standards but which today still leaves about one-third of its population living in poverty. This observation does not posit that debt has caused Kenya to realize a lower growth trajectory than expected. On the contrary, Kenya's growth trajectory may have been even worse with lower levels of debt. However, there is an evident missing link between debt and transformational growth in the case of Kenya and other African economies.

The second observation is that Kenya's vulnerability to both domestic and external shocks, where shocks are unanticipated events over which the economy has no control, means that borrowing becomes a burden instead of a route to economic prosperity. We document a recurrence of periods when public debt is increased aggressively in order to finance development, following ambitious government development plans, only for the progress to be derailed by periods during which shocks such as adverse weather conditions or global commodity prices increase external debt repayment obligations. This is illustrated, for example, by the occurrence of oil shocks in the late 1970s, which occurred when Kenya had a significant import bill due to the implementation of an ambitious infrastructure expansion strategy. A more recent occurrence, in the late 2010s, follows the expansion of fiscal spending to finance road and railway infrastructure that ultimately left the economy more vulnerable to a mix of shocks, including food and fuel inflation as a result of global wars, climate shocks and the COVID-19 pandemic. In these cases, where the room for additional debt financing is limited, the government implements fiscal consolidation policies to achieve a progressive reduction in the fiscal deficit and overall debt levels, but the mix of tax and expenditure policies weighs on short-term economic growth and typically has a more adverse impact on low-income households.

This observation highlights the interplay between the origination of debt for development and the incurrence of debt as a necessity to respond to negative shocks. History indicates that Kenya has followed cycles where it has over-committed in the origination of external debt to finance development without adequately accounting for the frequency and magnitude of shocks. The question arises if there is a failure of policymakers to "internalize" the costs of shocks that inevitably occur, and which are perhaps occurring with increasing frequency due to factors such as changing climactic factors. If so, there is a critical need to implement policies that improve the structural resilience of the economy to shocks and to provide adequate safety nets to cushion the most vulnerable households from shocks. Additionally, there is merit in structuring debt instruments to limit payments when shocks occur or in lowering the accumulation of debt in good economic times in order to limit the adverse impact of shocks.

A third observation is that developing economies often borrow in the currencies of high-income economies, making them more vulnerable to exchange rate shocks. The denomination of Kenya's external debt in foreign currency has proven to be a major contributing factor to debt fragility. As a consequence, global economic slowdowns exacerbate the severity of debt repayments when sudden financial flows, such as capital flight to safety, depreciate the value of the Kenyan shilling relative to the US dollar, which is viewed as the global reserve currency. Home bias also means that large pools of capital originating from advanced economies, including the United States, revert to their home economies, also tending to bolster their relative exchange rates. As the major share of Kenyan external debt is denominated in US dollars, debt repayment obligations deepen during crises. This includes concessional debt that is obtained for economic development from multilateral organizations such as the World Bank, which is denominated in foreign currency (US dollars), as is debt that is obtained from other sovereigns or raised from private sources of capital.

The rapid devaluation of the Kenyan shilling during the 1980s significantly increased debt repayment obligations on external debt, even though economic reform programs during this period extended concessional debt to aid in recovery from the global oil crisis. More recently, the Kenyan shilling experienced rapid depreciation in the 2020s as a consequence of increasing interest rates globally, leading to global portfolio rebalancing by international investors that resulted in capital outflows from developing and emerging economies, including Kenya, to advanced economies, resulting in the relative depreciation of the Kenyan shilling. However, of equal importance is the observation that principal and interest payments on servicing domestic debt account for the largest share of Kenya's total debt service payments. This reflects the relatively higher interest rates at which domestic debt is obtained relative to external debt.

These observations demonstrate the importance of limiting exposure to nominal exchange rate movements and also highlight the importance of deep markets for domestic currency debt. Advanced economies are less susceptible to exchange rate shocks because all or almost all of their public debt is denominated in domestic currency, including debt issued to non-residents. Their deep domestic markets also allow public sector borrowing at lower rates and without crowding out the demand for borrowing by the private sector. An immediate implication of these observations is to develop markets for domestic currency debt held by both residents and non-residents, including issuance of debt in domestic currency by regional development banks. Additionally, it highlights the major role played by exports, which not only serve as an engine for growth but also serve as an effective buffer against negative currency movements, thus allowing the economy to continue servicing its external obligations. Kenya's declining contribution of exports to growth since independence is a critical issue to be addressed, as it also negatively affects the economy's external debt carrying capacity. Also highlighted are the high costs imposed by external finance, including concessional finance, during global economic downturns, indicating the need to design these lending instruments more appropriately to mitigate the risk to borrowing economies.

Fourth, the issuance of external debt to Kenya has frequently been conditioned on the promotion of political and economic ideologies. This has been observed both at the bilateral level, which corresponds to debt agreements between Kenya and other sovereign nations, and the multilateral level, particularly relating to International Monetary Fund (IMF) and World Bank debt. The motivations behind creditors' conditions are driven by geopolitical considerations, including access to resources and creating global spheres of influence. These considerations do not necessarily coincide with the implementation of the best policies for the country. In fact, at the opposite extreme, in some African economies, geopolitical considerations have tolerated and reinforced poor levels of accountability within regimes with strong bilateral ties.

Fifth, Kenya pays a premium to access international commercial debt relative to countries in other regions of the world (excluding sub-Saharan Africa) that have a similar level of development. The premium paid for commercial debt is a subject of debate, with some policymakers and researchers ascribing a bias to lending terms, given that economies with worse track records of repayment are able to access international finance at more favorable terms. An opposing set of researchers ascribes the premium in capital markets to poor governance and transparency within Kenyan (and more broadly African) institutions. An important corollary of this observation is that beyond the obvious emphasis that must be placed on anchoring Kenya's institutions on a credible and transparent basis, the element of perception is critical and requires investment in projecting and safeguarding the safety of Kenya as a destination for private capital.

These key issues, among others, are explored in more detail within the book. The organization of the chapters begins with giving an account of some stylized facts regarding Kenya's public debt, and provides an understanding of global financial infrastructure. The subsequent chapters look at debt in the pre-colonial period, the colonial period and ultimately the period following Kenya's independence. The discussion of debt in the post-independence period is organized along economic reform ideologies, the impact of productivity and employment, the occurrence of shocks, and political economy considerations. Thereafter, the analysis looks at debt since the turn of the century, and explores the implications of the most recent developments with regard to the economy's public debt.

Notes

1 World Food Program (2022).
2 Fox and Jayne (2020).
3 The Asian Tigers include Hong Kong, Singapore, The Republic of Korea (South Korea) and Taiwan.

References

Fox, L., and T. Jayne. *Unpacking the Misconceptions about Africa's Food Imports*. Brookings Institute, December 14, 2020.

World Food Program. *Achieving Long-Term Food Security in DRC Is All about Building Resilience*. November 7, 2022.

1 Public Debt and the Global Financial Architecture

Our journey through the history of public debt in Kenya traces a period that begins with Kenya's pre-colonial era in the 1800s, shedding light on trade dynamics and dominant trends during this period that influenced the accumulation of debt in the coastal region under the control of the Omani empire and contrasting this region with the trends across communities in the interior geographical area that was later carved out as the Kenyan Republic. We thereafter describe debt dynamics during the colonial period, following the assertion of control by the British Empire over East Africa, and subsequently extend our discussion to the dynamics that followed with Kenya's participation in the global economy as a sovereign nation.

The composition of debt evolves across each period with shifts in global geopolitics and the consequent variation in the prominence of creditors, as well as the advancement of the global financial architecture. The composition of debt is discussed across some major dimensions that reflect the organization of markets for sovereign debt. First is the type of debt, where we distinguish between public debt and private debt. Public debt is either raised by the government or raised by entities that are guaranteed by the government, while private debt is raised by commercial entities. The majority of our focus is on public and publicly guaranteed debt, which raises a claim on every Kenyan citizen and which must eventually be repaid through tax revenues.

Overall, there are two types of public debt depending on the originating counterparty: external and domestic debt.[1] External debt includes amounts that are borrowed from non-residents and are denominated and payable in internationally acceptable currencies. There are three major types of external debt: bilateral, multilateral

DOI: 10.4324/9781003648826-2

and commercial. Bilateral debt is negotiated between two sovereign nations, while multilateral debt is borrowed from international organizations, including the International Monetary Fund (IMF) and World Bank, or regional banks such as the African Development Bank (AfDB). Governments frequently provide development aid through official development assistance (ODA), which includes grants, soft loans, or the provision of technical assistance to developing economies for the purpose of promoting economic development, with the funds channeled either bilaterally to the recipient or through a multilateral development agency. Commercial debt includes sovereign bonds with a maturity of one year or more that are raised on international capital markets under prevailing global financial conditions, or bank loans originated through contracts negotiated with private lending institutions, in many cases through syndicate lending.[2] Conversely, domestic debt is typically raised in local markets and in local currency and is majorly held by resident commercial entities, including commercial banks, insurance companies and pension funds.

A number of stylized facts are worth noting in understanding Kenya's debt dynamics. There are five distinct periods in the country's history of debt since the colonial era, which are in turn correlated with economic performance (Figure 1.1). Public debt was first originated in the colonial era, beginning with grants from the British government and evolving into debt raised from London that was guaranteed by the British government or borrowed directly from the Crown. The first multilateral debt also originated during this period. The colonial era was defined by tight controls on public debt and poorly developed markets for domestic debt, which resulted in a public debt profile dominated by external debt denominated in British pounds. In the next period following independence in 1963 through 1979, the country maintained a low and relatively constant share of debt in comparison to the size of the economy. In this period, Kenya experienced strong and sustained economic growth that averaged 7.1 percent, earning the country the reputation of a shining model to be emulated across the rest of Africa.[3] To date, the economic performance during this period remains Kenya's best in the post-independence era. The high levels of growth during this period were able to improve per-capita incomes despite high levels of population growth.

Thereafter, in the period that followed between the early 1980s and 1990, levels of debt increased rapidly in response to global economic shocks, in a context where the domestic economy also evolved

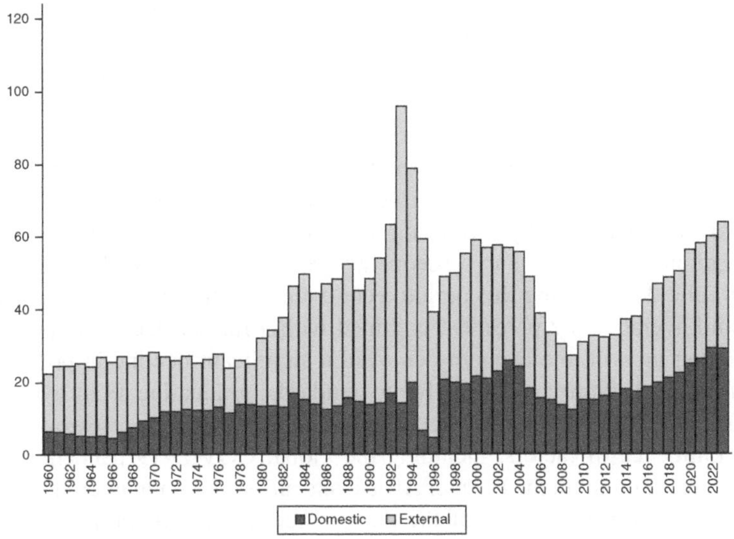

Figure 1.1 Domestic and external public debt (percent of GDP).

Source: Data from Kenya National Bureau of Statistics, Economic Surveys, 1970–2024. Official statistics from 1997 onwards include short-term borrowing.

with increasing employment in the informal sector, and where the domestic political environment also saw a deterioration in governance and accountability. In this period, Kenya was not alone in experiencing a major increase in debt, with similar trends observed in a large number of developing economies across the world. During the 1980s, Kenya's economic growth slowed significantly, and its development trajectory diverged at a faster rate relative to peer economies in Asia. Although population growth decreased somewhat during this period, the continued strong increase in population contributed to a slowdown in the growth of per-capita incomes.

In the subsequent period, between 1990 and the early 2000s, a deterioration of socio-economic indicators culminated in an economic crisis that resulted in macroeconomic reforms and debt restructuring.[4] The 1990s were the worst period in Kenya's post-independence economic performance, with growth averaging only 2.2 percent during the decade, including an economic contraction of 0.8 percent during the economic crisis in 1992, relative to a population growth rate of 3 percent. As a consequence, living standards declined, and there was a rapid increase in poverty. Global efforts targeted at restructuring debt, not only of Kenya but also of other developing economies, in addition to a rebound of the global economy, contributed to a decline in gross levels of debt at the turn of the century.

In the final period that we analyze, beginning in the early 2000s to the 2020s, Kenya was well poised for sustained growth. The economy was characterized by increasing levels of public investment in physical infrastructure that subsequently resulted in elevated levels of public debt. During this period, economic growth picked up steadily and averaged 5.2 percent. Combined with a further decline in population growth, the economy enjoyed a significant decline in poverty rates and improvement in living standards, graduating from a low-income economy to a lower middle-income economy. However, a confluence of factors, including the global COVID-19 pandemic, a severe drought in the Horn of Africa, and an escalation in international conflict, reversed some of the gains made during this period in the early 2020s.

Debt servicing payments have closely mirrored the evolution of debt levels, with payments of principal and interest mirroring the increase of public debt levels, as well as the mix between external and domestic debt (Figure 1.2). Payments of principal and interest on external debt can raise solvency issues as they are senior to other government expenditures, and the government has limited ability to use monetary tools to manage its external obligations relative to its domestic ones. Comparing debt servicing to government revenues gives an indication of the fiscal pressure exerted by debt obligations. A critical factor of note is that debt servicing on domestic debt accounts for the greatest share of debt servicing. This includes debt servicing in the 2010s, where the shares of domestic and external debt outstanding are almost equal, reflecting the fact that domestic debt is more expensive on average than external debt.

The period from independence through 1979 was characterized by low public debt servicing relative to central government revenues. Following this period, debt servicing obligations rose rapidly and peaked in the early 1990s when Kenya experienced debt distress. External payments arrears developed in 1991–92 for the first time in Kenya's history.[5] Debt servicing was dominated by repayments on domestic debt, reflecting the increasing cost of domestic borrowing

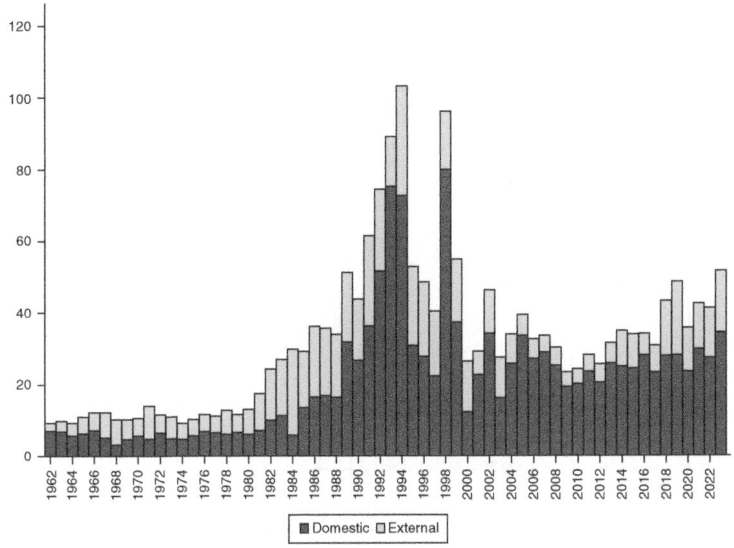

Figure 1.2 Public debt servicing (percent of central government revenues).
Source: Data from Kenya National Bureau of Statistics, Economic Surveys, 1970–2024. Domestic debt servicing in 1998 includes an overdraft.

and massive credit extended by the Central Bank, which fed into spiraling inflation that peaked at 46 percent in 1993. In the period from the 1990s onwards, payments on domestic debt have dominated debt servicing payments.

Debt restructuring subsequently led to a decline in debt servicing obligations. However, in the 2010s, debt servicing obligations rose again due to payments on borrowing for infrastructure. External shocks in the 2020s have led to a further increase in debt servicing and contributed to Kenya's classification as an economy at high risk of default.

Closely related to the structure and evolution of public debt is the question of defaults on outstanding debt and its impact on access to debt markets. The organization of debt markets and defaults at the global level provides a yardstick for Kenya's performance. Overall, the major distinguishing factor in the structure of global debt markets in the period leading up to the 1980s is the relative access to

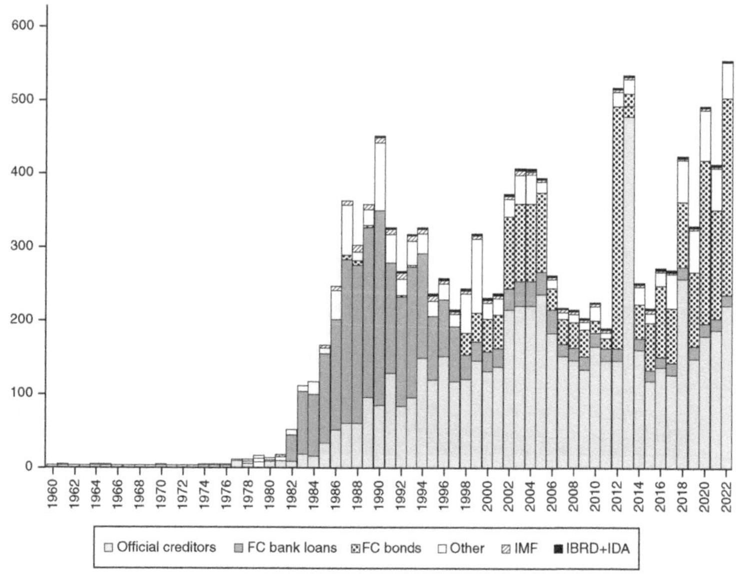

Figure 1.3 Global sovereign defaults (US$ billion).
Source: Data from Bank of England–Bank of Canada sovereign default database.

commercial debt across different regions. Latin American countries, which at this point were already relatively more developed than economies in sub-Saharan Africa (SSA), had significantly higher access to commercial debt markets, including both private commercial loans and international bonds, in contrast to the vast majority of African economies, which were limited to bilateral and multilateral sources of debt. Private commercial loans contributed a small share to overall debt in African economies. These differences in the structure of debt influenced the occurrence of defaults and the subsequent policy measures that were taken to address defaults in different regions of the world.

In the period between 1960 and 1980, defaults across the world were rare (Figure 1.3). During this time, global sovereign restructurings including defaults did not exceed a sum of US$20 billion in any given year. However, a dramatic shift occurred thereafter. The onset of the Mexican Crisis in 1982 resulted in large-scale defaults that topped US$450 billion by 1990, which amounted to 2 percent of global GDP during that year, the highest share of global economic output in the post-World War era.[6] The majority of global defaults in this period were foreign-currency bank loans, a significant share of which were held by US banks. Subsequent strong coordinated policy actions by the US government and loss provisioning by banks rapidly lowered the exposure of banks in the late 1990s. However, during the same period, the share of defaults to bilateral lenders that were members of the Paris Club increased, as did defaults on the growing market for foreign currency bonds, as well as defaults to other official creditors. Today, the major share of global defaults is on foreign currency bonds. In recent years, defaults to China have increased as it has gained prominence as a major bilateral lender to developing economies, but China's share of global defaults remains small.

Default patterns on loans from major multilateral lenders are also noteworthy. There were no defaults on World Bank debt in the 1960s or 1970s.[7] The first defaults are triggered in the 1980s and grow to above US$1 billion by the end of the decade. In comparison, a number of defaults on lending by the IMF occurred in the 1960s and 1970s, particularly by economies in Latin America, including Argentina, Brazil and Uruguay.

Kenya's pattern of debt repayments stands in contrast to the major global trends. Critically, Kenya has never defaulted on multilateral debt owed to the IMF or the World Bank. However, Kenya has had loans cancelled from bilateral partners and private creditors. The history of debt servicing reveals a period of 20 years following independence during which the occurrence of restructuring was infrequent and limited to low amounts. However, a shift occurred thereafter with a greater frequency and magnitude of restructuring. In the period between the mid-1980s and the mid-1990s, the economy experienced a combination of challenges between the global fallout from the Mexican Crisis that began in 1982 and domestic governance and accountability problems that eventually resulted in a sudden halt in foreign lending. During this period Kenya restructured funds borrowed from private creditors and official creditors. In the period between 1987 and 1990, Kenya wrote off US$627 million in external debt.[8] Thereafter, in 1994, the Paris Club cancelled US$535 million of Kenya's outstanding debt.[9] At the turn of the century, Kenya entered an agreement with the IMF to implement a poverty reduction and growth facility arrangement, whereby the implementation also included the restructuring of outstanding external Paris Club debt and commercial debt, with the objective of creating fiscal space to support economic recovery. In November 2000, the Paris Club announced an agreement with the Government of Kenya to reschedule a total of US$300 million, of which US$111 million comprised principal and interest of maturing ODA loans, US$166 million comprised commercial debt, and the remainder consisted of arrears.[10] Subsequently, Kenya agreed to a rescheduling of US$350 million of Paris Club debt in January 2004.[11]

In 2021, as a consequence of debt fragility after Kenya's sustained build-up of debt outstanding with infrastructure investments and the impact of the COVID-19 pandemic, the country entered into the Debt Sustainability Suspension Initiative that resulted in the suspension of debt repayments on a net present value neutral basis, including the participation of both Paris Club members and the People's Republic of China, which was Kenya's largest bilateral creditor. With the debt suspension, a 4-year maturity extension was granted in addition to a 1-year grace period extension.[12]

These stylized facts paint a picture of Kenya's debt dynamics, as well as the frequency with which the government has restructured its debt obligations. However, an understanding of public debt in Kenya and other developing and emerging economies is incomplete without a description of the global financial architecture, which illustrates the distribution of debt across developing and high-income economies, how the composition of debt—including access to concessional and commercial debt—changes with the level of economic development, the critical role played by credit rating agencies in the issuance of commercial debt as well as in influencing the structure of multilateral debt, the major incentives that countries have to service external debt, and the factors that influence debt renegotiations and restructuring.

It is striking that public debt in low-income and lower middle-income economies accounts for only 6 percent of global public debt, with the debt of low-income countries alone accounting for less than 1 percent of global debt. Public debt in the United States alone, which accounts for 34 percent of the global total, is almost three times as much as the debt of more than 70 economies. At the same time, low and lower middle-income economies account for almost half of the world's population. Thus, despite contributing a small share of global debt, public debt in these economies has far-reaching implications for almost 4 billion individuals across the world.

Due to low domestic savings, developing economies borrow internationally and have a debt profile that is composed of both domestic and external debt. The structure of debt by income indicates that, on average, low-income economies have a higher share of external debt, lower middle-income economies have roughly equal shares of domestic and external debt, and upper middle-income economies have a higher share of domestic debt.[13] Domestic debt in local currency is desirable due to its lower vulnerability to external shocks, and also by virtue of serving as a benchmark for other debt issuance that supports the growth of domestic markets. However, in recessions, governments may be tempted to print currency to pay down existing domestic debt, eventually spurring inflation and resulting in a real transfer from investors to government. Realizing this, rational investors price in this risk and raise the cost of domestic borrowing. In contrast, external debt in foreign currency does not expose creditors to this risk. Additionally, the use of domestic savings to finance public debt can lead to the crowding out of private sector lending, which can ultimately have a negative impact on economic growth.[14] Thus, both domestic and external debts have advantages and disadvantages for creditors and borrowers.

The structure of external public debt varies according to the level of development. Low-income economies have a major share of concessional debt from multilateral organizations, as well as a large share of bilateral debt. However, these economies are for the most part unable to access commercial debt, either in the form of bank loans or sovereign bonds, which account for a small percentage of total debt. The share of commercial debt increases with the level of development, with lower middle-income economies, including Kenya, able to issue sovereign bonds. Commercial debt accounts for the majority of debt in upper middle-income economies, which also have a low share of bilateral debt.

The external public debt in low- and lower middle-income economies is denominated in international currencies, and mostly in US dollars. In contrast, almost all public debt in high-income economies, including debt held by non-residents, is denominated in local currency, which reduces susceptibility to foreign exchange risk. In particular, multilateral debt issued by organizations including the IMF and World Bank is denominated in US dollars and contributes a significant share of external debt to developing economies. Multilateral organizations frequently issue debt on concessional terms, and this debt is treated as senior to all other international debt claims and domestic public liabilities. These organizations are able to extend concessional terms in part by borrowing cheaply from international debt markets due to their credit ratings, rated at triple-A—the highest possible level—by credit ratings agencies. However, maintaining high ratings creates major incentives for these organizations not to renegotiate on outstanding liabilities in cases of fragility or distress and also incentivizes borrowing economies to prioritize debt repayments to multilaterals in order to maintain access to cheap debt. As a consequence, debt-induced economic crises can cause major economic hardship when economies choose to maintain debt repayments at the expense of providing public services. High levels of poverty in developing economies mean that millions of individuals are left especially vulnerable, and, in many cases, a minor share of global debt under distress ends up exerting disproportionately large social costs and pushing many additional individuals into poverty.

The growth of sovereign bond markets led to the emergence of a critical role for credit rating agencies, which are institutions that undertake due diligence and provide information on the default risk of sovereign issuances. Due to the private information that a sovereign has on its ability to pay, a lender must either exert effort directly to monitor the quality of the sovereign or rely on third-party risk assessments from independent ratings agencies. Credit ratings are especially important for internationally issued sovereign bonds and play a major role in determining the risk premia that investors demand on sovereign issuances. In contrast, issuers of privately placed loans frequently perform their own due diligence. Policymakers in SSA often flag mispricing of debt as a key concern due to an unjustifiable perception of risk within international financial markets that results in higher risk premia in comparison to other continents.

For developing economies that can access debt from commercial markets, there is mixed evidence on risk premia that are paid on sovereign bonds across different regions of the world. Evidence shows that governments in SSA pay about 2.9 percentage points more to borrow from international financial markets than other economies and also that herding behavior occurs among international investors resulting in mispricing due to discriminatory behavior rather than macroeconomic fundamentals.[15] Economies in SSA are found to pay significantly higher coupons on debt upon issuance and also to pay higher refinancing costs in the secondary market. However, opposing research finds that the excess premium paid by African economies in international debt markets is explained by structural factors including the transparency of budget processes, the level of financial development and the quality of public institutions.[16] Analytical frameworks used to assess debt sustainability are also subject to significant uncertainty, and the information investors rely upon may not accurately reflect the likelihood of default. For example, the IMF's debt sustainability analysis, which is a globally monitored standard of modeling a country's public debt levels and repayments over time, is recognized to systematically underestimate debt trajectories over the medium term.[17]

There is no international enforceable mechanism to ensure that nations repay sovereign debt, and so the question arises why lending to sovereigns occurs in the absence of a clear legal framework. There are two major reasons: first, a country has the incentive to maintain a good "sovereign reputation", thus signaling its quality by making payments on debt in good times to ensure it can continue to access financing during an economic downturn or during a period of economic distress.[18] And second, a creditor may have the ability to exert "direct punishment", where the creditor exerts a high cost on a defaulter by seizing its assets, excluding the defaulter from participating in credit markets, or restricting the defaulter's access to international trade markets.[19] This is supported by the significant effort and detail that go into specifying legal clauses within contracts that provide leverage to creditors.[20] For instance, clauses in sovereign bonds waive immunity from execution, permitting a creditor to execute on sovereign commercial assets even where there is no link between the asset and the loan. Additionally, legal rights in a specific jurisdiction can make lending by alternate creditors within the same jurisdiction more difficult. For example, the enforcement of clauses in the case of default may recognize the claims of affected creditors as senior over the issuance of any new credit, thereby discouraging the extension of any loans by commercial entities within the same jurisdiction.

An analysis of sovereign debt restructurings over a period of 200 years shows that restructurings are costly to private creditors, with losses from defaults amounting on average to about 45 percent of the face value of debt in the event of restructurings.[21] Debt restructurings that are pure reschedulings, where the maturity of debt is extended without a reduction in face value, are also fairly common. However, full repudiations in which 100 percent of debt is written off are highly uncommon, occurring in exceptional circumstances such as major geopolitical events including wars or revolutions. Further, countries that depend on domestic debt are less likely to default than those depending on external debt.

If a country defaults, evidence shows that it is more likely to experience growth if the "haircut" on default, that is, the loss incurred by the creditor in the event of default, is steeper. Thus, interim restructurings that do not enable a country to exit a debt spell are associated with a decline in growth, relative to final restructurings that cure default, which are associated with an increase in growth.[22] Additionally, the defaulting country and creditor are likely to be better off if the negotiation is brief. However, negotiation processes typically include multiple interim defaults and restructurings because the parties do not initially recognize the need for deeper haircuts. This may stem in part from wrongly identifying solvency crises as liquidity crises, whereby the misdiagnosis assumes the inability to pay is temporary and due to unfavorable short-term conditions that are unlikely to persist, as opposed to structural issues that require restructuring in order to enable the country to meet its long-term obligations. There is also evidence that preemptive restructurings result in lower output losses, and thus a country with a high likelihood of debt distress is likely to experience the best outcome by entering debt negotiations early and negotiating a sufficiently deep discount.

These characteristics of the global financial infrastructure expose Kenya and other developing economies to risks but also facilitate the availability of international finance for development. However, it is evident that urgent global efforts are needed to improve global debt instruments and reduce the vulnerability of developing economies to economic shocks that exert major social costs on the developing world.

Notes

1 There are three possible definitions of external and domestic debt, which focus on the currency in which the debt is issued, the residence of the creditor, or the place of issuance. Official compilers of statistics on debt focus on residency, where external debt is owed to non-residents (Panizza, 2008).

2 A syndicate loan is offered by a group of lenders that jointly provide credit to a large borrower.

3 Economic and population growth data are obtained from the World Bank's World Development Indicator database.

4 See IMF (1995), p. 1.

5 See IMF (1995), p. 1.

6 Global sovereign default statistics are obtained from the Bank of Canada and Bank of England sovereign defaults database. The database considers debt to be in distress—and effectively in default—when an interruption in scheduled debt service occurs, a sovereign seeks to renegotiate the existing contract terms of any of its obligations or a combination of both.

7 Concessional (low interest) debt and grants are issued by the World Bank's concessional lending arm, the International Development Association (IDA), which was established in 1960 and which complements the World Bank's original lending arm, the International Bank for Reconstruction and Development (IBRD). Loans provided by IDA carry zero or very low interest rates, and payment terms are over 30–40 years. Historically, IDA has been funded by contributions from member country governments, who meet every three years to replenish resources and review the policy framework. See https://ida.worldbank.org/en/what-is-ida.

8 See Ngeno (2000), p. 135.

9 Debt restructuring data for Kenya are obtained from the Bank of Canada and Bank of England sovereign defaults database.

10 Paris Club Press Release, *The Paris Club and Kenya Agree to a Debt Restructuring* (November 15, 2000).

11 Paris Club Press Release, *The Paris Club Agrees to a US$ 350 million Debt Restructuring for Kenya* (January 15, 2004).

12 See Paris Club, "Kenya Debt Treatment: Agreement on the Debt Service Suspension Initiative (DSSI)", January 11, 2021; https://clubdeparis.org/en/traitements/kenya-11-01-2021/en.

13 World Bank (2021).

14 Diamond (1965).

15 See Olabisi and Stein (2015); Morsy and Mustafa (2020).

16 See Gbohoui et al. (2023), Gueye and Sy (2015).

17 See IMF (2017).

18 This approach was first pioneered by Eaton and Gersovitz (1981).

19 This approach is developed by Bulow and Rogoff (1989).

20 Weidemaier and Gulati (2017).

21 Luckner et al. (2023).

22 Forni et al. (2016).

References

Bulow, J., and K. S. Rogoff. "A Constant Recontracting Model of Sovereign Debt." *Journal of Political Economy* 97, no. 1 (1989): 155–78.

Diamond, P. A. "National Debt in a Neoclassical Growth Model." *The American Economic Review* 55, no. 5 (1965): 1126–50.

Eaton, J., and M. Gersovitz. "Debt with Potential Repudiation: Theoretical and Empirical Analysis." *The Review of Economic Studies* 48, no. 2 (1981): 289–309.

Forni, L., Palomba, G., Pereira, J. and C. Richmond. *Sovereign Debt Restructuring and Growth*. IMF Working Paper WP/16/147, 2016.

Gbohoui, W., Ouedraogo, R. and Y. M. Some. *Sub-Saharan Africa's Risk Perception Premium: In the Search of Missing Factors*. International Monetary Fund Working Paper WP/23/130, 2023.

Gueye, C. A. and A. N. Sy. "Beyond Aid: How Much Should African Countries Pay to Borrow?" *Journal of African Economies* 24, no 3 (2015): 352–366.

International Monetary Fund. *Kenya Recent Economic Developments*. Report No. SM/95/289, 1995.

International Monetary Fund. *Review of the Debt Sustainability Framework in Low-Income Countries: Proposed Reforms*. IMF Policy Paper, August 2017.

Luckner, C. G., J. Meyer, C. Reinhart and C. Trebesch. *Sovereign Debt: 200 Years of Creditor Losses*. Working Paper, 2023.

Morsy, H., and E. Moustafa. *Mispricing of Sovereign Risk and Investor Herding in African Debt Markets*. Working Paper Series No. 331, African Development Bank, 2020.

Ngeno, N. "The External Debt Problem of Kenya". In *External Debt and Capital Flight in Sub-Saharan Africa*, eds. S. Ajayi and M. Khan, 2000.

Olabisi, M., and H. Stein. "Sovereign Bond Issues: Do African Countries Pay More to Borrow?" *Journal of African Trade* 2, no. 1–2 (2015): 87–109.

Panizza, Ugo. *Domestic and External Public Debt in Developing Countries*, Discussion Paper No. 188, United Nations Conference on Trade and Development, 2008.

Weidemaier, M. C., and M. Gulati. "Sovereign Debt and the 'Contracts Matter' Hypothesis". In *Oxford Handbook of Law and Economics*, 2017.

World Bank. *Assessment on Public Sector Domestic Debt*. Debt Statistics Team, World Bank Development Data Group, 2021.

2 Debt in East Africa during the 1800s

In the 1800s, finance in East Africa was dominated by Indian merchants based primarily in Zanzibar, who controlled trade in ivory and slaves and also financed the growth of plantations along the East African coastline that grew commodities, including cloves, sugarcane and grain. They also provided advances to the Sultan of Oman, who had moved his seat of power to Zanzibar and who claimed sovereignty over the region, and were delegated the authority to collect customs duties on behalf of the Sultanate, thus consolidating their position of power over trade. Their provision of finance to caravan expeditions looking for ivory and slaves was critical to the flourishing of trade during this period. Further, inland trade among communities was dominated by barter, which implied the immediate settlement of transactions. However, cloth was also used as a medium of exchange, and cowrie shells and the Indian rupee were also used for transactions, although the use of currency was uncommon. Overall, private finance dominated this period, and the emergence of public finance did not occur until the dawn of the colonial period.

By the 1800s, the Industrial Revolution was in full swing, and blossoming industries in Europe and the Americas increased their demand for input raw materials. Industrial development was in turn reliant on labor, where labor demand varied according to the level of mechanization across industries. Africa increased in prominence as a source of both raw materials and labor. In particular, the demand for labor incentivized an increase in slave trade and saw a major uptick in East African slavery, with slaves forced to work on plantations at the coastline, in addition to being sold abroad. Ironically, the increase in slavery occurred during a period when liberal ideology had taken a

DOI: 10.4324/9781003648826-3

powerful foothold in Europe, following the occurrence of watershed events such as the French Revolution in 1789.

The demand for ivory in Africa increased dramatically during the early 1800s, with the ivory trade having a devastating impact on the continent's elephant population. African elephants dwindled from a population of 26 million in 1800 to less than 1 million in the 2010s,[1] and the continent continues to struggle with ivory smuggling despite a worldwide ban on ivory sales in 1989. The ivory frenzy was driven by its use in a variety of products ranging from billiard balls and piano keys to jewelry. East Africa's ivory, in particular, was recognized as superior in quality relative to South-East Asian ivory and easier to work with in carvings, given it was both softer and bulkier.[2] It was also understood to be abundantly available at low cost to enterprising individuals willing to trade within the East African plains.

The commercial trade in ivory became the most important activity in East Africa, outstripping the slave trade and other commercial activities, and was supported by an elaborate trade network. Arab vessels already had well-established trading routes that for centuries had connected cities on the African coast to the Middle East and Asia, facilitating intercontinental trade. The ivory trade already existed on a smaller scale going back centuries before. Marco Polo, the famous Venetian explorer, remarked of the East African coast as far back as the 13th century, "they have elephants in plenty and drive a brisk trade in tusks".[3] Ivory trading networks grew dramatically when Zanzibar was established as the capital of Oman, occurring when Sayyid Said, ruler of the Kingdom of Oman, relocated from Muscat in 1832.[4] Sayyid Said relocated his throne to Zanzibar to counter the threat of Arab families that had been increasing their power and influence along the East African coast, thereby prompting an increase in the Arab and Indian population in Zanzibar. Plantations were established in Zanzibar to grow cloves, as well as along the East African coastline to produce commodities including grain and sugar. These plantations were labor-intensive and therefore the major drivers of the slave trade within the region.

Sayyid Said imported the economic framework established in Muscat to drive commercial trade in East Africa, thereby placing Indian financiers at the center of the ivory trade. Indian merchants invested their capital in loans to Arab, Swahili and European merchants and established dominance in import and export trade in Zanzibar. A critical factor that enabled this level of control was the position that influential Indian merchants enjoyed as collectors of customs duties on behalf of the Omani Sultanate, a practice that was highly valued and which was assigned through bidding rights. The collection of duties in turn allowed Indian merchants to exert control over the movement of goods along the coast and provide favorable treatment to commercial allies.[5] Further, shrewd merchants extended credit to the throne and, therefore by keeping the kingdom in a state of perpetual debt, were able to maintain control of customs operations. The most important and well-known customs master in Zanzibar was Jairam Shivji, who amassed wealth by extending credit to Arab and Swahili-led caravans, as well as lending to western firms.

Colonel Hamerton, who arrived in Zanzibar as British Consul in 1841, remarked that trade in ivory and slaves was controlled by Indian merchants.[6] Although Indian merchants were frequently described as mere brokers, their status was illustrated by Sir Bartle Frere, who remarked in 1973,

> Everywhere, wherever there is foreign trade, it passes through the hands of some Indian trader; no produce can be collected for the European, American or Indian market but through him; no imports can be distributed to the natives of the country, but through his agency ... It is difficult to convey to those at a distance an adequate idea of the extent or completeness of the monopoly.[7]

Indian domination of finance continued until the turn of the century, at which point it was estimated that as of 1905, Indians controlled up to four-fifths of capital and business in British East Africa. However, in the 1900s, the British began to exert more direct control over the East African coast and instituted settler self-government, which in turn implemented increasingly anti-Asian legislation that curbed the influence of Indian finance.[8]

The nerve center of capital that financed commercial activity in East Africa was Surat, in India, which was the center of Gujarati trade under the Mughal Emperors. Gujarati bankers, often Vania by caste and Hindu or Jain by religion, had gained significant capital by virtue of benefiting from East Asian trade, particularly from exporting raw cotton and opium to China, as well as exporting cotton to the West.[9] The movement of capital from India to East Africa was facilitated by the use of Bills of Exchange, written orders binding one party to a contract to pay a fixed sum to the other party on demand or at a predetermined date. Although trade in Zanzibar and Mombasa was controlled by Indians, Arabs played a more modest role as moneylenders further up the Kenyan coast in Lamu.

The ivory trade led to the development of well-defined trading routes within the territories of Kenya and Tanzania, although trade extended much further south into Malawi and Mozambique. The major trading routes passed through Tanzania and terminated at the port of Mombasa, although the northernmost route traversed the Kenyan plains below Maasai-controlled territory through Moshi and Arusha, before turning upwards toward Lake Victoria. This journey took 55 days by caravan.[10] Arab-controlled caravan routes dominated Tanzania in large part due to the multiple points of resistance they faced in Kenyan territory, where the communities were stronger and more aggressive than those in Tanzania and where communities were also warier of engaging with foreigners. In large part due to the Maasai, communities in the Kenyan highlands were insulated from Arab interaction, particularly in the first half of the 19th century. The Maasai were frequently hostile to caravans and gained a reputation that discouraged traders from venturing into Maasai-controlled territory. It was not uncommon for well-armed expeditions to get wiped out by sudden attacks from the Maasai.[11] Within Kenya, the ivory trade was controlled by the Akamba, who already had well-established relationships with their neighboring communities in the Kenyan highlands and who formed the trade link between these communities and the Kenyan coast. This control was reinforced by the fact that indigenous communities did not display much interest in trading with caravaneers. Kitui rose in prominence as a regional exchange center that supported long-distance trade with the Kenyan coast.[12]

As a consequence, the most devastating consequences of the ivory and slave trade were endured by Tanzania, extending into the lake regions, into Uganda and Central Africa, where larger and more established kingdoms experienced major shocks. Those kingdoms that participated in the ivory and slave trade gained greater wealth and influence than their neighbors and also grew in power by gaining access to weapons, particularly from western traders. Two great inland markets for ivory grew in Tabora in central Tanzania and Ujiji on the east coast of Lake Tanganyika.[13] As growth in the ivory trade grew, competition emerged between the established routes that gravitated around the control of Zanzibar and trading routes that grew on the river Nile, passing through Sudan into Egypt, and which were financed by the Egyptian governor Muhammad Ali.

Ivory expeditions grew in size with demand, to the extent that by 1885 it was not uncommon to have over 2,000 porters in a single caravan.[14] Indian merchants established themselves as the backbone of finance for these expeditions. Arab caravans obtained goods to trade inland on credit, which were in turn used to barter for ivory. In the 1800s, cotton cloth was the most important manufactured commodity brought into East Africa, which was also controlled by Indians.[15] However, the American market also became influential as trade in *Merikani*, a white and inexpensive cotton from America, occurred alongside other fabrics, including *Dobwani*, a desired fabric from Muscat. Other goods in high demand included beads, although these were sensitive to shifts in fashion that influenced the color of beads demanded.

Unlike finance at the coast, trade with inland communities was frequently conducted on the basis of barter. Arab caravans found that livestock was highly valued in exchange for ivory and increasingly resorted to raiding communities for livestock during expeditions in order to obtain cattle to trade for ivory. Ivory tusks varied significantly in size, ranging from a few pounds to over 200 pounds. It was also difficult to find a perfect pair of tusks, given that elephants typically favor the use of one tusk over the other, resulting in more wear and tear on the oft-used tusk. To transport the ivory back to the coast, which in many instances was bulky, heavy and awkward to carry, caravans depended on professional porters hired at the coast or slaves hired out by their masters. Merchants also used slaves captured or bought from inland communities to transport ivory and thereafter sold the slaves themselves at the coast.

Ivory expeditions were risky and expensive. Rates of interest on trade goods, including ivory, reflected the dangers involved in carrying caravan expeditions, including the high level of insecurity as well as the duration over which it was necessary to extend credit. Caravan leaders frequently contracted to sell the spoils of their trips to lenders at discounted rates in a form of trade credit. These preferential purchase agreements also underpinned Indian finance in other parts of the coast, such as diving seasons for pearls in the Red Sea and the Persian Gulf. The financial risks of expeditions were reflected by extremely high interest rates charged to Arab caravaneers, sometimes as high as 100 percent. Colonel Hamerton remarked that the Indian merchant "gave credit to the Arab caravan leader in the form of trade goods and was repaid at enormous rates of interest in the form of ivory and slaves".[16] Indian financiers were paid in ivory, other products obtained from trade, or with Maria Theresa Thalers obtained from the sale of slaves, where the Thaler, the currency of the Austrian empire, was an unofficial currency in some parts of Africa and Asia.

With regard to plantations in Zanzibar and along the coast, Indian financiers secured their loans on harvests from plantations and, over time, increasingly extended loans on the value of the plantations themselves. In cases of default, rather than foreclosing on land, the financiers preferred to purchase future harvests at preferential rates. The significance of influential Indian financiers grew to the extent that as of 1873, Jairam Shivji's business had over £140,000 outstanding in loans and mortgages to Europeans and Americans. The authorities also played an important role in upholding the execution of all contracts. For example, a judge upheld the high interest rate charged by an influential Indian financier, Tarya Topan, on the famous Arab caravan leader, Tippu Tib, as justified by the risks involved.

In contrast to the wealth of written records documenting long-distance trade between inland communities and the coast, written accounts of trade among communities in Kenya are limited. Unlike coastal cities, a strong oral tradition was the basis upon which information was recorded, shared among individuals and codified for future generations. Therefore, a historical account of trade and the nature of debt in inter-communal trade in the 1800s is necessarily incomplete due to the sparse availability of reliable information during this period. While an authoritative discourse is impossible, and any attempt at an exposition inevitably raises more questions than answers, it is possible to shed some light on how debt was likely perceived during this period and what its implications were within society.

Some general considerations must preface any discussion. Within communities, events of particular significance were recognized through the practice of important rituals. Although the oral tradition was rich, inconsistencies in information about past events tended to occur with time. Further, when written accounts eventually began to be recorded by foreign travelers, their records were not based on scientific and systematic methods and were frequently biased by the motives of the authors. Thus, accurate and consistent statistics recorded over time from these sources do not exist over this period, and there are wildly differing accounts of events depending on the source of information.

Unlike long-distance trade between inland communities and the coast, trade among inland communities was to a large extent determined by geographical diversity and by climate. Those communities that lived in fertile areas within the highlands practiced intensive agriculture. Research on agricultural production gives differing accounts of the magnitude of production, with some accounts emphasizing self-sufficient and subsistence-oriented production and other accounts emphasizing surplus production for the purpose of trade.[17] For example, the Embu engaged in agriculture supported by the significant and reliable rainfall on the slopes of Mount Kenya, while further west the Kisii also engaged in farming sustained by arable land and dependable rainfall. Bordering intensive farming, neighboring communities receiving less rainfall engaged in mixed farming, accumulating cattle in addition to cultivating crops, and pastoralist community livelihoods were dictated by semi-arid conditions unsuitable for intensive farming, but where the vast expanse of available land supported cattle rearing.

Communities developed different mechanisms to deal with vulnerability to adverse climate. Pastoralist communities accumulated large herds to provide a buffer against drought and traded cattle with communities that practiced intensive agriculture in order to allow them to focus their labor on cattle-rearing. Pastoralists used cattle as a store of value, and cattle were readily acceptable as a commodity by farming communities in exchange for produce, in addition to holding significant value for cultural ceremonies in some communities, such as marriage traditions. Their cattle buffers allowed pastoralists to trade for surplus foodstuffs during drought periods. Herd sizes grew and diminished in accordance with weather patterns, serving as a form of insurance against climate shocks. In cases where a herd of cattle was lost, historical accounts document that pastoralists would offer labor in exchange for food.[18] There were also conflicts across different communities and within clans in the same community occasioned by climate shocks, the expansion of areas for cultivation and disease. In some cases, the impact of climate shocks was devastating, as detailed by famine records from the mid-to-late 19th century.[19] For example, one particularly extreme famine in 1898–99 is estimated to have caused the death of 30 percent of all Kamba.[20]

A vibrant inter-communal trade was established on the basis of barter. By its nature, barter suggests the immediate settlement of a claim where an exchange of goods proportionate to a negotiated value occurs across the transacting parties. Therefore, in trade among farming and pastoralist communities, the most frequent mechanism did not depend on the extension of credit. In addition to barter, cloth was used as a medium of exchange, and although the use of currency was not common, there was also trade in the Indian rupee and cowrie shells. It is documented that trade among some communities, such as the Kisii and the Luo, was mainly conducted by women as they were more capable of traveling across territories unmolested to ad-hoc marketplaces that met one to several times a month.[21] The predominance of barter trade suggests that debt was not a significantly developed instrument that facilitated trade among inland communities to the same extent that long-distance trade between inland and coastal communities was facilitated by international financial networks. Certainly, historical accounts of trade across communities do not emphasize the extension of credit.

The social and political organization of communities across Kenyan territory also offers insight into the likely conceptualization of debt within communities. Along the Kenyan coast, the thriving cities were under the direct control of the Omani kingdom. However, most inland communities were to a large extent smaller and organized in a politically decentralized manner, with the exception of the Kingdom of Wanga. A common thread across these societies was their highly egalitarian nature. The majority of societies were "chiefless", where no recognized royal lineages existed and each member was accorded equal status. This societal organization served as an effective counter-balance to the rise of high levels of inequality that create conditions under which structural borrowing and debt can become embedded within society.

This recognition was reinforced by the manner in which society was organized and governed. Government was structured such that every individual not only had the opportunity but also the moral obligation to participate actively in its day-to-day administration. The constitution of government was based on age groups that determined levels of authority, participation and division of responsibilities. The council of elders held the highest level of authority and was the seat of decision-making and dispute resolution. In principle, within the class of elders, every member enjoyed equal recognition in terms of authority, and decisions were made on the basis of consensus. Men of singular ability were bound to exist and would be afforded outsized political influence, but their status was based on ability and was neither hereditary nor authoritarian.[22] Other age groups had greater responsibility for the provision of labor and defensive protection to the community, and the youngest uninitiated individuals carried no formally recognized responsibility or authority.

Under this horizontal system of government, the accumulation of wealth was not a viable option to consolidate or reinforce status or galvanize the organization of society into a wealth-based hierarchy. At the extreme, the risk that accumulated surplus could be redistributed within the community during the occurrence of shocks probably created counter-incentives to expend energy to produce significantly beyond an individual's needs. The communal nature of society also discouraged the enumeration of assets. It was considered taboo and discourteous to enumerate one's belongings, and social norms actively discouraged accurate enumeration. During Kenya's first census, implemented in 1948, it was noted, "East Africa is peopled with inhabitants to whom the expression of quantities is not considered important. There is 'a lot' (Mingi) or 'a little' (Kidogo) but a definite measurement is a bad thing". A further description adds, "With other tribes, to count anything is courting the disfavor of the gods, and although the African will know each of his cattle or goats by name or color he will never say and never will admit knowing the total numbers".[23]

Property rights within agricultural communities were defined communally, and there was no concept of individual land ownership. Land was accessible to those members of the community with the need and means to cultivate it. Any land that was underutilized could be assigned to those without land. In this way, every member of the community was guaranteed access to an area within which to create a livelihood. Any strain on resources that arose as communities grew was naturally resolved through expansion, which required effort to clear and cultivate forested areas. As a result, communities spread apart geographically over time, creating distance. The thin and horizontal structure of government meant that the locus of control diminished with distance, loosening bonds and creating new loosely connected clans in the process. By their nature, pastoralist communities were more dispersed and grazed their cattle on the vast tracts of territory controlled as a community.

Neither did a system of taxes exist in society until the hut tax was implemented during colonial rule in 1901. This precluded the concentration of wealth for public services within an administrative structure and did not allow its potential administrators to leverage its existence for power. In contrast, subsequent administrative structures show how dramatic changes in power dynamics were able to occur in a short period of time. For example, colonially appointed chiefs were able to exert power on society by virtue of acting as local agents of the colonial government, frequently overshadowing the power of the existing structures and becoming de facto lawgivers.[24]

It is important to note that historical accounts give a polarized picture of life among inland communities in traditional Kenyan society. On the one hand, society is portrayed as egalitarian, sedentary and utopian, with a strongly embedded sense of community, shared resources and low inequality. On the other hand, society is described as highly vulnerable to famine and disease, which frequently resulted in intertribal conflict due to competition for resources. These extremes posed a risk to population growth, and it is unclear whether communities experienced a slow, steady increase in population or an overall decline due to these factors. Accounts of Kenya's population during this time are sparse and inconsistent. However, guesses have been made by various explorers and administrators who visited East Africa. These were subject to significant margins of error. For instance, Sir Arthur Harding estimated the population of Kenya in 1897 to be 2.5 million, while Portal thought that the population could not have exceeded 450,000.[25] The authors did not use any methods apart from observation and did not attempt to persuade readers that these estimates were anything but guesses.

Toward the end of the 19th century, the dynamics of both coastal and inland communities changed dramatically as a consequence of rapidly shifting geopolitical shifts that prompted the British government to exert direct control over East Africa, culminating with the establishment of a colony by the turn of the century. British global influence grew following the conclusion of the Napoleonic wars in 1815, when British debt was at the highest level in its history, having surpassed 200 percent of GDP.[26] Following the Napoleonic wars, Britain experienced a period of relative peace during the remainder of the 19th century. Fiscal prudence, in addition to the economic boost provided by the Industrial Revolution, allowed the economy to grow out of debt, with British debt declining to 30 percent of GDP by the turn of the century. During this period of globalization, British dependence on raw material imports for manufacturing increased sharply, with imports of tin, copper, lead and zinc rising to 80 to 100 percent of production inputs before World War I.[27] This period of structural transformation also increased Britain's dependence on agricultural imports from its colonies while at the same time it cultivated these as markets for both goods and capital exports.

Britain had a policy of financing wars through the accumulation of debt and thereafter increasing taxes to pay off debt, effectively following a tax-smoothing policy. During war, the government would issue unfunded debt through a variety of short-term obligations, including exchequer bills. Longer-term securities were issued following war periods, funded by specially earmarked indirect taxes and therefore cheaper, in order to retire the unfunded debt. The origin of the term "funded debt" originated from the issuance of permanent loans in the 1600s, where the State was under no obligation to repay the principal amounts borrowed but agreed to the payment of interest forever or up to any such time that the principal may be repaid. This was in contrast to "unfunded" or temporary loans, where the State undertook to repay the principal at a fixed date.[28] The credibility that the British were capable of paying back accumulated debt was supported by its parliamentary system, where debt-holders exercised considerable influence and therefore protected their interests.[29] This tax-smoothing policy was efficient from the perspective that wars constituted a short-term shock and played a key role in rapidly ramping up finance for war campaigns, thereby decisively influencing the eventual outcomes.

The completion of the Suez Canal in 1867 resulted in a major increase in the interest of other European powers in Eastern and Southern Africa. The canal dramatically decreased the trading distance between Europe and the East African coastline and also spurred greater activity by explorers and missionaries, who in turn contributed to painting a more vivid picture of the region's potential. At this point in time, Britain enjoyed a trade and commercial monopoly over the Indian Ocean. Britain exerted its influence over the East African coast indirectly through its influence on the Sultan of Zanzibar, who claimed sovereignty over Eastern Africa, even though his influence was limited to the coastline and he had no effective control over the interior. The British were able to enjoy this special political influence over the Sultan by means of providing continued support in disputes with Arab rivals.

The British reacted to the increasing interest of other European powers in the region by electing to increase the Sultan's dependence on the Crown, anticipating that in turn this would create a significant barrier against other powers gaining influence in the region. A two-pronged strategy was employed by Sir John Kirk, who became the British Consul-General in 1873, by providing military support to the Sultan while at the same time reducing the influence of the powerful Arab-Swahili trade along the coastline. Kirk arranged the appointment of a British naval officer, Lloyd Matthews, to establish a standing army for the Sultan.[30] At the same time, the slave trade was employed as an effective instrument to weaken Arab-Swahili influence. Kirk progressively used military and diplomatic pressure to oppose the slave trade, which underpinned the strength of the Arab-Swahili plantation economy along the coastline. It was through British lobbying with the Sultan that the East African slave trade was abolished in 1873, eight years after slavery was abolished in the United States. However, the British did not enforce an outright ban in an attempt to manage confrontation along the coast.

The effectiveness of this approach proved to be limited. Other European powers, and in particular Germany, took an active interest in East Africa and initiated a campaign to establish agreements with African leaders in the region. German attempts were successful in creating a foothold within East Africa. Across the continent, the rush by imperialist powers to consolidate their influence over different regions prompted diplomatic efforts in order to avoid confusion and the risk of conflict over spheres of influence within Africa, culminating with the Berlin Conference in 1884–1885. This series of meetings consolidated imperialist control and the resultant fate of Africa. In particular, Germany's move into East Africa prompted the British Empire to re-evaluate its actions in order to protect its interests in the region, including control of the River Nile at its source, given its importance to Egypt. Following the conference, Germany signed a delimitation of spheres of influence with Great Britain in 1886.

Britain's policy thereafter shifted to supporting private sector-led development of the region under its influence, with the British government continuing its reluctance to exercise direct control and directly incur administrative expenses and responsibility. The Crown supported the incorporation of the Imperial British East Africa Company (IBEA) by William Mackinnon in 1888, which was in turn given the mandate to develop trade in the East African areas controlled by the British

Empire.[31] The Sultan of Zanzibar signed a concessional agreement with the IBEA that gave over all rights of administration and power that he possessed over the mainland to the company. Administration was, however, carried out in the Sultan's name and subject to his sovereign rights.

Part of the British Empire's rationale for providing administrative rights to the IBEA was the massive expanse of the empire, which was already stretched in capacity while trying to develop the territories it had claimed in Southern Africa. It therefore favored exercising any mode of indirect control and was more than happy to grant the necessary rights to the company. However, IBEA's existence was short-lived. It found that administration of the colony was far more expensive than anticipated and had little by means of income. It also found active resistance to establishing a presence in the interior, for example, when the Kikuyu destroyed Fort Lugard. By 1895, it was evident that the company would be unable to continue as a viable concern, and its fate was sealed with the sale of its assets to the British government. Growing British interest in East Africa culminated in the establishment of the East African Protectorate in 1895, thereby ushering in the next phase of British control of the territory.

Notes

1 National Geographic, "The History of the Ivory Trade"; https://education.nationalgeographic.org/resource/history-ivory-trade/.
2 Beachey (1967), p. 269.
3 Beachey (1967), p. 269.
4 Srinivasan (2000).
5 Clarence-Smith (2001), p. 342.
6 Beachey (1967), p. 277.
7 Frere (1873), p. 101–2.
8 Clarence-Smith (2001), p. 338–39.
9 Clarence-Smith (2001), p. 342.
10 Beachey (1967), p. 271.
11 Abir (1968), p. 107.
12 Ambler (1985).
13 Beachey (1967), p. 272.
14 Beachey (1967), p. 273.
15 Clarence-Smith (2001), p. 339.
16 Beachey (1967), p. 277.

17 For example, Hakannson (1994) discusses surplus production for the purposes of trade.
18 See Hakansson (1994), p. 269, which states, "warfare, famine and disease dispersed communities and forced people to seek food and protection in other clans".
19 Nilometer readings, which are historical records of water levels in the River Nile, provide accurate corroborating evidence on the occurrence of these events (see Hartwig, 1979, pp. 658–59).
20 Hartwig (1979), p. 658.
21 Hakannson (1994), p. 262.
22 Tignor (1971).
23 East African Statistical Department (1948).
24 Tignor (1971), p. 341.
25 Martin (1949), p. 303.
26 Wright (1999), p. 355.
27 Wolff (1970), p. 273.
28 Cox (1901), p. 360.
29 Bordo and White (1991), p. 304.
30 Bordo and White (1991), p. 452.
31 Bordo and White (1991), p. 458.

References

Abir, M. "Caravan Trade and History in the Northern Parts of East Africa." *Paideuma* 14 (1968): 103–20. www.jstor.org/stable/40341453.

Ambler, C. H. "Population Movement, Social Formation and Exchange: Central Kenya in the Nineteenth Century." *The International Journal of African Historical Studies* 18, no. 2 (1985): 201–22. https://doi.org/10.2307/217740.

Beachey, R. W. "The East African Ivory Trade in the Nineteenth Century." *The Journal of African History* 8, no. 2 (1967): 269–90. www.jstor.org/stable/179483.

Bordo, M. D., and E. N. White. "A Tale of Two Currencies: British and French Finance During the Napoleonic Wars." *The Journal of Economic History* 51, no. 2 (1991): 303–16. www.jstor.org/stable/2122576.

Clarence-Smith, W. G. "Indian and Arab Entrepreneurs in Eastern Africa (1900–1914)." *Publications de la Société française d'histoire d'outre-mer* (2001): 335–49.

Cox, H. "The Public Debt of Great Britain." *The North American Review* 173, no. 538 (1901): 355–76. www.jstor.org/stable/25105214.

East African Statistical Department. "East African Population Census 1948: Some Problems of Planning." *The American Statistician* 2 no. 4 (1948): 17–18. www.jstor.org/stable/2682686.

Frere, B. *Memorandum by Sir B. Frere Regarding Banians or Natives of India in East Africa.* British Parliamentary Papers, 1873.

Hakansson, N. T. "Grain, Cattle, and Power: Social Processes of Intensive Cultivation and Exchange in Precolonial Western Kenya." *Journal of Anthropological Research* 50, no. 3 (1994): 249–76. www.jstor.org/stable/3630179.

Hartwig, G. W. "Demographic Considerations in East Africa during the Nineteenth Century." *The International Journal of African Historical Studies* 12, no. 4 (1979): 653–72. https://doi.org/10.2307/218071.

Martin, C. J. "The East African Population Census, 1948. Planning and Enumeration." *Population Studies* 3 no. 3 (1949): 303–20. www.jstor.org/stable/2172580.

Srinivasan, P. "Indian Traders in Zanzibar with Special Reference to Jairam Shewji (19th Century)." *Proceedings of the Indian History Congress* 61 (2000): 1142–48. www.jstor.org/stable/44144429.

Tignor, R. L. "Colonial Chiefs in Chiefless Societies." *Journal of Modern African Studies* 9, no. 3 (1971): 339–59.

Wolff, R. D. "Economic Aspects of British Colonialism in Kenya, 1895 to 1930." *The Journal of Economic History* 30, no. 1 (1970): 273–77. www.jstor.org/stable/2116744.

Wolff, R. D. "British Imperialism and the East African Slave Trade." *Science & Society* 36, no. 4 (1972): 443–62. www.jstor.org/stable/40401672.

Wright, J. F. "British Government Borrowing in Wartime, 1750–1815." *The Economic History Review* 52, no. 2 (May 1999): 355–61. www.jstor.org/stable/2599943.

3 Debt during the Colonial Period

Kenya's first issuance of public debt occurred during the colonial period, which covered the duration between 1895 and 1963. Over the course of colonization, there were shifting patterns in debt issuance that established the structure of public debt that was inherited by independent Kenya. With the establishment of the East Africa Protectorate, grants-in-aid were the primary source of finance to support the administration of the East African territories. The colony then shifted to borrowing directly from the Imperial Treasury and thereafter was able to access capital markets in London, where an implicit guarantee by the Crown lowered the cost of access to debt. Over this period external debt markets developed significantly, while in contrast, there was limited development of domestic debt. The major interest of private banks with a local presence was to finance trade, and they had limited interest in supporting the issuance of domestic colonial bonds. In the 1950s, Kenya also accessed multilateral finance for the first time with a loan from the World Bank. Additionally, major controls were implemented during the colonial period to manage the accumulation of public debt under the principle of self-sufficiency of imperial territories. Thus, public debt was well managed as a matter of necessity during this period, even though the extractive nature of colonialism meant that public investments were targeted at benefiting British settlers as opposed to developing the economy for all Kenyans.

The East Africa Protectorate (also known as British East Africa) included the area from the coast up to Lake Naivasha, while the area further west to Lake Victoria and further to the Congo border became the Uganda Protectorate, with a Foreign Office Commissioner put in charge of the administrative affairs of each territory.[1] In order to

DOI: 10.4324/9781003648826-4

support the administration of both territories, the Imperial Treasury began contributing annual grants-in-aid in the order of £200,000 for British East Africa and £150,000 for Uganda. The first grant was provided to the East Africa Protectorate in July 1895, and grants would be provided for the next 18 years, up to 1913. In total, grants-in-aid received from the Imperial Treasury to British East Africa over this period totaled £2,843,383.[2] Grants-in-aid were provided as an exception to territories where the administration of law and order was not possible without causing an impossible strain on the domestic budget. In general, the principle that guided the administration of any territory was that it should "have only those services which it can afford to maintain out of its own resources".[3] The widely held view was that the development of territories should not exert any costs on the British taxpayer. As a consequence, when approved, grants-in-aid came with the condition of very strict control of a territory's finances by the Imperial Treasury, frequently discouraging enough that governors did all they could to raise domestic revenues before requesting grants-in-aid. As part of the conditions to receive a grant, a territory was required to submit detailed expenditure estimates for advance approval by the Imperial Treasury, with justification for each expenditure heading within its budget. Additionally, approval was necessary for any variations from approved estimates.[4]

The protectorates were transferred from the Foreign Office to the Colonial Office in April 1905, with the boundary of British East Africa extended to Lake Victoria, coinciding with the boundaries of Kenya at independence.[5] As a protectorate, the legal status was such that the territory was treated as foreign and therefore not part of the British Empire, and where the authority of the Crown extended by virtue of agreements with "local chiefs or headmen", as stated by the Foreign Jurisdiction Act, 1890. As a consequence, the provision of funds from the Treasury was frequently met with friction in parliamentary debates, as British funds were not fully secured. This was superseded in 1920 when the Colony of Kenya was established through the annexation of the East Africa Protectorate to the British Dominions. The colonial period brought about a radical transformation in the organization of society and transitioned the territory of Kenya from the web of interconnected but independent communities into the Republic of Kenya as it is organized today.

British interests in East Africa resulted in the commissioning of the Uganda Railway, beginning in 1896. The name of the railway is noteworthy for the simple fact it highlights just how little regard the British gave to the value of Kenyan territory at this point. The mapping of the railway was planned to provide the most direct possible route between Mombasa and Lake Victoria. The Uganda Railway was Kenya's first major infrastructure project and first external investment. From its inception, construction of the railway faced fierce criticism in London and piqued the interest of the British taxpayer because it was to be financed not by debt but directly through British taxes. In one of the debates in British parliament, a member emphasized the demerits of the railway as "starting from nowhere and going nowhere". The construction of the railway was initially estimated to cost 3 million British pounds.[6] At that point in time, the cost of the railway amounted to about 0.15 percent of British GDP, not an insignificant amount given the expanse of the empire and the sum total of its obligations.[7] However, the railway eventually ended up costing over 5.5 million British pounds (approximately equivalent to KES 65.5 billion in 2022), almost double the initially anticipated cost. Construction of the railway was completed at Kisumu, then known as Port Florence, in December 1901. The length of the completed railway measured 937 kilometers.

It is remarkable how much cheaper the Uganda railway was relative to the modern Standard Gauge Railway (SGR), whose construction began in 2013. The SGR was designed to run parallel to the Uganda railway, which was a narrow-gauge railway, and was financed through debt from the Government of China. The total estimated cost of the SGR is KES 800 billion once completed,[8] 12 times as expensive as the Uganda railway measured in inflation-adjusted terms. While admittedly there are major differences in the cost of labor employed for construction, the use of technology and the type of railway gauge, the difference is striking.

The Uganda railway faced fierce criticism within the United Kingdom in part because it was an anomaly relative to the imperialist mode of operation. Globally, British control over imperialist interests underwent a series of evolutionary shifts over time. At first, the core aim was to extract resources, with the view that colonies were rich sources of precious metals. This was short-lived due to shifting global attitudes towards the exploitation of foreign lands, as well as disappointing returns in many of the territories relative to the costs of administration. Attitudes thereafter shifted to supporting the development of financially self-sufficient colonies with minimal debt, save for minor exceptions. Augmenting this was an extended view of commerce, where the colonies were seen not only as sources of raw materials for British industry but were also to be developed as markets for the benefit of the United Kingdom, with transport to be monopolized by British ships. The view that colonies should be self-governed, with the British Empire given access as a preferential trading area, subsequently developed later in the twentieth century.[9]

The self-sufficiency model meant that discussions on colonial policy were generally given low priority within British parliament. As one astute observer noted: "Hardly anything bores or empties the House of Commons as colonial policy does—until, as a result of that policy or lack of it, a colony blows up and provides the opportunity for party political capital".[10] The Uganda railway elicited a strong reaction precisely because of its controversial nature, with a large constituency arguing that the strategic concerns behind its construction did not justify the required capital outlay.

The railway had a major although initially unforeseen impact on opening up inland trade. The massive cost overruns during construction and the high subsequent maintenance costs motivated colonial authorities to develop trade that would increase the level of self-sufficiency within the territory and lower its dependency on the Crown. In particular, the potential for agriculture within the highland regions came to be recognized, and efforts were expended to encourage British settlers to develop large-scale farming. The newly constructed railway revolutionized access between inland areas and the coast; relative to the caravans that dominated interior trade prior to its construction, the railway decreased transportation times and increased trade volumes by an order of magnitude. In fact, one of the arguments advanced for the construction of the railway was that it would displace the caravan trade and effectively bring the slave trade to an end. Rail branches were constructed to high-potential agricultural areas, and Nairobi, which initially came into existence as a post during the construction of the railway, grew in prominence.

Settlements were encouraged as a consequence of the railway. The colonial government turned to a policy of providing incentives for British expatriates to deploy their capital to develop agricultural land. This was coupled with the encouragement of commercial banks to open branches in Kenya to provide private sector lending. The colonial government supported the forced displacement of local communities in the most fertile regions in Kenya in favor of European settlement. The justification for displacement was provided by the enactment of British laws. Prior to the annexation of British East Africa, control over land was exercised after the promulgation of the Crown Lands Ordinance in 1902, which provided the British with the authority to issue outright sales of land or leases for a period of 99 years. According to the ordinance, when land was no longer occupied by Africans, it could be sold or leased as if it was unoccupied, with no requirement for obtaining the agreement of any representative of a given tribe. The 1915 Crown Lands Ordinance went further by defining Crown Land to include land occupied by natives. This ordinance increased agricultural leases to 999 years but kept town leases to 99 years. As a consequence of these leases, which conferred secure tenure of land to settlers, the agricultural sector grew and formed a base on which to impose both direct and indirect taxes. Kenya grew its trade with a focus on exports, and the major source of government revenue was extracted from import and export taxes, in addition to excise and sales taxes.

Additional laws were enacted to force the supply of cheap local labor. The hut tax, the first tax exerted over the East African Protectorate, was introduced in 1901 following the completion of the railway. This tax introduced for the first time a widespread notion of liability to the state across inland communities in Kenya by imposing a mandatory cash payment that was levied on all able-bodied adults. This represented a major shift from pre-colonial cultural norms. The tax was far from sufficient in generating income to cover the administrative expenses of the territory as the tax base in the country was small, but it created an incentive for individuals to work on farms established by European settlers. Besides the hut tax, it is also worth noting that at an individual level, access to finance for locals was particularly challenging and highly restricted by law. The 1903 Credit to Natives Ordinance stated that no credit of more than £10 could be advanced to an African without the approval of a District Officer.

The hut tax also increased the utilization of currency in the economy, as it was the medium by which taxes were demanded and paid. The major currency in circulation in East Africa at this time was the Indian rupee, which was used in conjunction with other instruments of barter trade, such as cowrie shells. The Indian rupee was made the standard coin for the East Africa Protectorate in 1898. In addition, the government minted copper cents that were circulated in addition to currency previously introduced by the IBEA. Africans mostly held copper cents due to the low economic value of their transactions.

The Indian rupee was made of silver, and therefore its value fluctuated with global commodity prices. These market fluctuations were the source of major conflict between settler farmers and commercial banks, where the colonial administration, acting in support of the farmers, attempted on multiple occasions to limit losses arising from market movements by fixing the exchange rate between the sterling pound and the Indian rupee, or by selectively limiting losses to cents, which would have disproportionately impacted the African community. Following disputes and lobbying of the British Crown by both sides, the East African shilling was introduced in 1922 and pegged at a value of one-twentieth of the pound sterling. This stood as the Colony's official currency until independence.

As revenues grew in the Protectorate with the expansion of agriculture, the government transitioned to borrowing loans from the Imperial Treasury as grants-in-aid came to an end. The growth of lending to British colonies was supported by the Colonial Loans Act of 1899, which permitted the provision of loans to develop infrastructure for exports in colonies, thereby lowering the likelihood of future grants to colonies. Loans from the Imperial Treasury were justified by the inability of the colonies to access capital markets directly on their own account.[11] In advancing the East African Protectorates Bill and justifying the provision of loans to the colonies, The Secretary of State for the Colonies, Lewis Harcourt, stated in Parliament, "As will be seen from the provisions of the Bill, arrangements are made for the repayment of these loans, both as to capital and interest, by the Protectorates themselves, at no cost at any time to the British taxpayer".[12] He further stated:

> The fact is, that production in these countries has altogether unexpectedly outstripped the carrying capacity of the countries. There is naturally a great congestion, both on the railways and lakes and at their seaports, which very naturally leads to complaint—justifiable complaint from those who have to deal with the production. If goods cannot get to the coast there is a grave danger that in the immediate future the cultivation of many articles may cease.[13]

These loans were defined by a number of key characteristics. First, issuances were tied directly to the completion of specific infrastructure developments. And second, the loans were issued with the implementation of sinking funds, instruments that committed the government to ring-fence funds over a period of time in order to guarantee repayment of the loans. The Finance Act of the United Kingdom of Great Britain and Ireland, 1911, advanced the first loan of £250,000 from the Imperial Treasury to the East Africa Protectorate for the purpose of improving the railway and harbors, as well as providing piped water supply in Mombasa.[14] In 1913, an additional £375,000 was secured from the Imperial Treasury for the purpose of further improvements to the railway and Lake Victoria ports, the purchase of a cargo steamer and improvements to the terminal facilities at Kilindini. The terms of the loans were an interest rate at 3.5 percent, as well as a sinking fund at 1.5 percent.[15]

Additionally, the framework was laid in place that allowed the colony to access unsecured debt directly from London. Beyond direct lending, an important element of the British Empire was the access that colonies had to London's capital markets. In most colonies, domestic capital and money markets were underdeveloped and the colonies relied heavily on the London market. Therefore, although this meant that local banking conditions as well as the base of local deposits were not a meaningful constraint to access to debt, it also meant that the development of indigenous financial markets suffered as a result.[16] Ease of access to the London capital and money markets was of considerable value to the colonies. There was an implicit guarantee of debt by the British government, which lowered premiums for borrowing relative to other economies. The Colonial Stock Act of 1900 gave trustee status to colonial issues and was one reason for the high standing of colonial loans. Other reasons for the low interest rates were that over a long time, no colonial government had defaulted, there was a belief that the British government would act to prevent any defaults and there were fairly large sinking funds provided. Thus, it is thought that colonial bonds may have been subjected to liquidity risk, but not to credit risk, given the implicit credit guarantee given by the sovereign.[17]

The General Loan and Inscribed Stock Ordinance, 1921, gave the Colony of Kenya the authority to raise capital through debentures with the debt charged upon the general revenues of the colony and required the creation of sinking funds for the redemption of the debentures.[18] Further, the ordinance gave the governor the authority to convert debentures into inscribed stock or to issue inscribed stock, in accordance with the provisions of the Colonial Stock Act, 1877. Inscribed stock meant that ownership of stock was recorded through entry on the Bank of England's books, which constituted the sole, legally binding evidence of a stockholder's assets. There were no stock certificates, and although receipts were issued to stockholders, these were not legally binding. Similarly, sales and transfers were also recorded in the bank's books. This centralized but unwieldy system of record-keeping meant that it was imperative that accurate records be maintained and that the records be kept safe.

The colony raised £5,000,000 of debt in 1921, at an interest rate of 6 percent, redeemable over the period 1946–56. Sinking fund contributions were set to commence no later than 3 years from the date of issue, with contributions at a rate not less than 1 percent.[19] As a consequence of broader access to debt in London, the capacity of the colonial government to borrow increased significantly and issuance of debt in London became a prominent component of public debt. The Colony consistently and increasingly raised financing from London over time, except during World War II (Table 3.1). The tenure of stock issuance was generally above 20 years.

Table 3.1 Inscribed stock issuance by the Colony and Protectorate of Kenya

Year of Issuance	*Amount Issued*	*Interest Rate*	*Redeemable*	*Price of Issue*
1921	5,000,000	6.00	1946–56	95.0
1927	5,000,000	5.00	1948–58	99.5
1928	3,500,000	4.50	1950	95.0
1930	3,400,000	4.50	1961–71	98.5
1933	305,600	3.50	1957–67	98.5
1936	375,000	3.00	1956–61	100
1945	600,000	3.00	1970–75	100
1946	1,820,000	2.75	1971–76	99.0
1947	3,710,000	2.50	1965–70	99.0
1951	6,070,000	3.50	1973–78	100
1952	6,115,000	4.25	1971–78	99.5
1953	6,510,000	4.25	1971–78	100
1954	2,925,000	4.00	1960–61	100
1955	2,500,000	5.00	1970–72	99.0
1956	4,225,000	5.00	1978–82	96.0

Sources: Kenya Colony and Protectorate Annual Report (1933), p. 48, and IBRD (1961), Table 1.

The East Africa Currency Board (EACB), which was established in December 1919, had a major influence on the debt profile of the Kenyan economy during the colonial period. The currency board was established following a similar concept to currency systems that once operated in Burma, India and Ceylon (which later became Sri Lanka) and was the second currency board established in Africa after the West African Currency Board in 1912. It was, in effect, a sterling exchange system where a currency authority issued local currency in exchange for sterling pounds at a fixed rate. The authority did not have any discretionary authority over issuance and was required to stand ready to redeem any and all amounts between sterling and the local currency to an unlimited amount as required by demand. This was the analogue to a gold standard, but one that was based on the sterling pound and its ability to maintain its global status.

The EACB was required to hold more than 100 percent in sterling currency reserves to support its ability to execute currency exchange transactions on demand. Initially, the Board controlled the currency of the Kenya Colony and Protectorate and the Uganda Protectorate but grew to include other countries, the first of which was Tanganyika in 1920, after a League of Nations mandate had been given to the United Kingdom to administer this territory following the conclusion of World War I. Zanzibar subsequently joined in 1936, and following military operations in 1942–43, Somaliland, Ethiopia and Eritrea also joined. Ethiopia's stay was short-lived, and it left in 1945 to begin issuing its own currency.[20]

Despite its mandate, the Board could only manage a fraction of the reserve requirement upon its inception and only eventually reached 100 percent coverage over 30 years later, in 1950. The lowest coverage was in 1932,[21] following the Great Depression, when reserves dropped to only 10 percent of the currency in circulation and prompted the colonial governments of Kenya, Uganda and Tanganyika to pass legislation that guaranteed coverage of the reserve fund gap, in effect promising to borrow from London to honor any large simultaneous redemptions into sterling.[22] The Great Depression occurred in 1929 and lasted for almost a decade, constituting one of the worst economic downturns in modern history. It was marked by steep declines in industrial production, deflation and mass unemployment, affecting a large number of countries globally. One of the key events that precipitated the depression was the collapse of the United States stock market, ending a period of speculation where stock prices had risen to unprecedented levels. Additionally, the gold standard played a role in spreading the impact of the crisis to other parts of the world, especially Europe. As the American economy contracted, so did its demand for imports, which resulted in the United States running trade surpluses with other countries. This in turn gave rise to foreign gold outflows to the United States, thereby depleting gold reserves in trading partners. Other economies responded by raising interest rates, which had the effect of reducing domestic output.

In the midst of the Great Depression, the British government took steps that increased its commitment to developing its colonies, in part because of the hope that this would stimulate growth and bring relief to the mass levels of unemployment during the Depression. The 1929 Colonial Development Act introduced a commitment to provide funds to colonial governments, with a sum of £1 million per annum made available for capital works. Across colonies, priority was given to those that promised the best rates of return. The Colonial Development and Welfare Act of 1940 increased the allocations to £5 million per annum. Following the end of World War II, the Colonial Development Corporation, which was subsequently renamed the Commonwealth Development Corporation, was established in 1947 with the power to borrow up to £150 million from the Exchequer for project finance.[23]

Within the EACB, part of the reserves were held in cash in order to satisfy immediate demand for redemption, but the majority were invested in income-earning securities of different maturities, mostly concentrated in gilt-edged securities that were easily redeemable on the London market. All EACB investments were restricted to the London market until 1955, even though the EACB was not expressly restricted from making local investments by its regulations. Nevertheless, it followed what was then the accepted practice of other territories until 1955, when their regulations were amended. Further, the EACB's interactions were almost exclusively with commercial banks, although it had the authority to deal with any person that met certain minimum requirements per transaction.

Until 1955, the EACB was, in practice, a highly controlled system that limited the capacity of colonial governments to implement any monetary policy. Colonial governments did not have the discretion to control the money supply, and the EACB system took the place of a local central bank or reserve bank. Thus, in effect, the colonial government faced severe monetary constraints absent in countries with independent monetary and banking systems. The fixed exchange rate effectively made the Kenyan economy an extension of the British economy.

The strict monetary environment meant that any excess of expenditures over revenues had to be met by external revenues or funds, as the government did not have the authority to "print" money. This also contributed to inflationary stability. As of 1952, the EACB held a total of GBP 35 million in investments, all in British government securities. The lack of developed financial markets locally also meant that government surpluses and reserves of various types, such as marketing funds and pension funds, were invested in London. In addition, commercial banks invested their funds into British securities, given the absence of domestic debt markets and their lack of interest in local government bonds. Thus, Kenyan assets were effectively lent at very cheap rates to the British government instead of being deployed for domestic development. In fact, the lending was effectively free until 1951, as no distribution of interest from the reserve funds was made before then.

The oppression of Kenyans by the colonial government led to the Mau Mau uprising, which began in 1952 as a movement that targeted independence. The consequence of the uprising was a serious escalation in conflict between the colonial authorities, settlers and Africans, which led to the declaration of a state of emergency and military operations to contain its protagonists. The rebellion was disruptive to economic production and international confidence, and Kenya was unable to raise loans in the London market from 1956.[24] Over time, as the security of tenure of white settlers became increasingly uncertain, capital outflows began to increase. The increasing financing gap prompted the colonial administration to increase its demand for loans and grants directly from the United Kingdom and also to approach multilateral organizations for their assistance.

The Colony of Kenya began accessing multilateral loans in the 1950s. The first loan by the International Bank for Reconstruction and Development (IBRD), the lending arm of the World Bank, was made to the East Africa High Commission, a statutory body that was established in 1948 for the purpose of controlling and administering services common to the Colony and Protectorate of Kenya, the Trust Territory of Tanganyika and the Protectorate of Uganda. A loan of US$ 24 million was secured for 20 years at a rate of 4 ¾ percent in 1955 with the payment of principal and interest guaranteed jointly by the governments of all three territories, as well as by the United

Kingdom. This loan marked the beginning of US dollar-denominated multilateral debt. The purpose of the loan was to cover part of the costs incurred in the development and administration of railways and harbors in East Africa.[25]

Following this loan, the IBRD extended a loan to the Colony of Kenya in 1960 for an amount of US$ 5.6 million dollars for the development of agriculture and transport infrastructure. The loan documents were signed in Washington, DC, by the Ambassador for Great Britain in Washington, Sir Harold Caccia, on behalf of the United Kingdom and the Colony and Protectorate of Kenya, and the loan was guaranteed by the United Kingdom.[26] The loan was made in support of the Swynnerton Plan, which began in 1955, in order to increase the production of crops and livestock and whose purported objective, following the Mau Mau civil unrest, was to increase living standards, particularly for African farmers. The terms of the loan were 10 years at an interest rate of 6 percent, including a 1 percent commission to the World Bank's Special Reserve. A grace period of 3 years was given before amortization began in January 1964. Thereafter, a loan of US$8.4 million was obtained from the IBRD in 1962 to support the land resettlement program that was agreed upon following the termination of the Mau Mau emergency. The program, known as the Million-Acre Scheme, was devised to purchase 200,000 acres of European-owned mixed-farming land each year over a five-year period for the purpose of resettling Africans. This program continued through independence and became one of the major initial expenditures of the independent government.[27]

Although imperial banks and other large commercial banks began operating in Kenya in the 1890s, they played only a minor role in public finance. The National Bank of India began operations in 1896, followed by the Standard Bank of South Africa in 1910 and the National Bank of South Africa in 1916.[28] The major business of commercial banks was the financing of export and import trade, and the banks had limited interest in supporting local colonial government bond issues. As far as commercial banks were concerned, colonial governments were on the same footing as private customers.

Following Kenya's independence in 1963, the authorities made concerted efforts to develop the country's domestic markets for both public and private finance, laying the foundations for the modern financial infrastructure that exists today. These actions shifted Kenya away from dependence on British financial infrastructure, although the United Kingdom remains to date one of Kenya's central development partners.

Notes

1 Leggett (1915), p. 212.
2 East Africa Protectorate Annual Report for 1913–1914, p. 7.
3 Stammer (1967), p. 195.
4 Stammer (1967), p. 195.
5 Leggett (1915), p. 213.
6 The estimate adjusts the cost by inflation as measured by the CPI. Data from the Bank of England Quarterly Bulletin, 1994, and World Bank WDI Database.
7 The United Kingdom's real GDP in 1900 was £154 billion in 2017 prices (£2 billion in nominal terms).
8 Kazungu S., "SGR costs to add up to Sh800bn after phase 2 deal signed," *Business Daily*, August 21, 2018. The costs include KES. 327 bn for the Mombasa-Nairobi phase, KES. 150 bn for the extension to Naivasha, and KES. 380 bn for the final phase terminating in Kisumu.
9 Stammer (1967), p. 192.
10 Stammer (1967), p. 192.
11 See British Parliament Hansard; https://api.parliament.uk/historic-hansard/commons/1914/apr/07/east-african-protectorates-bill#S5CV0060P0_19140407_HOC_289.
12 See British Parliament Hansard; https://api.parliament.uk/historic-hansard/commons/1914/apr/07/east-african-protectorates-bill#S5CV0060P0_19140407_HOC_289.
13 See British Parliament Hansard; https://api.parliament.uk/historic-hansard/commons/1914/apr/07/east-african-protectorates-bill#S5CV0060P0_19140407_HOC_289.
14 United Kingdom of Great Britain and Ireland, Finance Act, 1911, Chapter 48, Section 16(2).
15 See East Africa Protectorate Annual Report, 1913–14.
16 See East Africa Protectorate Annual Report, 1913–14, p. 200.
17 See East Africa Protectorate Annual Report, 1913–14, p. 196.
18 General Loan and Inscribed Stock Ordinance (1921).
19 Colony and Protectorate of Kenya Annual Report (1933), p. 48.
20 Kratz (1966), p. 229.
21 In 1932, £EA 3.6 million pounds were in circulation (Kratz 1966, p. 232).
22 The guarantee covered the reserve fund gap up to £EA 1.5 million (Kratz 1966, p. 232).
23 Stammer (1967), p. 197.
24 IBRD (1961), p. 5.

25 IBRD (1955).
26 See IBRD Press Release No. 634, May 27, 1960.
27 Shaffer (1967), p. 127.
28 Ochieng et al. (1990), p. 254.

References

Colony and Protectorate of Kenya. *General Loan and Inscribed Stock Ordinance No. XVII of 1921*. 1921.

Colony and Protectorate of Kenya. *Annual Report on the Social and Economic Progress of the People of the Kenya Colony and Protectorate, 1933*. Report No. 1688, 1934.

East Africa Protectorate. *Report for 1913–1914*. Report No. 840, April 1915.

International Bank for Reconstruction and Development. *Appraisal of the East African Railways and Harbours Administration Development Program*. Report No. T. O. 70-a, February 25, 1955.

International Bank for Reconstruction and Development. *Current Economic Position and Prospects of Kenya*. Report No. EA-118, August 7, 1961.

Kratz, J. W., "The East African Currency Board." *International Monetary Fund, Staff Papers* 13, no. 2 (1966).

Leggett, Major E. H. M. "The Economic Development of British East Africa and Uganda." *Journal of the Royal Society of Arts* 63, no. 3246 (1915): 209–20. www.jstor.org/stable/41341935.

Ochieng W. R., and R. M. Maxon. *An Economic History of Kenya*. July 1990.

Shaffer, N. Manfred. "Land Resettlement in Kenya." *Yearbook of the Association of Pacific Coast Geographers* 29 (1967): 121–39. www.jstor.org/stable/24042329.

Stammer, D. W. "British Colonial Public Finance." *Social and Economic Studies* 16, no. 2 (1967): 191–205. www.jstor.org/stable/27856263.

4 Independence and the Development of Debt in the Early Years

Independent Kenya inherited public debt that was dominated by external claims mostly to the United Kingdom and poorly developed markets for domestic debt. The infrastructure financed by public debt was concentrated in developing European settlement areas principally for agricultural exports, in addition to the administration of the colony and the oppression of Kenyans, especially during the Emergency period in the 1950s. Public debt upon independence was modest relative to the size of the economy, but the legitimacy of these claims remains in question given that the majority of debt was not originated for the benefit of all Kenyan citizens. Following independence, the government diversified its sources of external finance by increasing borrowing from other bilateral partners as well as increasing borrowing from multilateral organizations, thus changing the profile of external debt and increasing the share of claims in US dollars. The World Bank eventually became Kenya's most significant external creditor. Key national institutions were created that supported the development of domestic markets for debt, including the Central Bank of Kenya and the National Social Security Fund. Additionally, the government purchased major shareholding in the country's largest banks and contributed to growing the domestic financial sector. Through these deliberate efforts, domestic debt grew to account for half of Kenya's public debt after independence.

By the late 1950s, it was evident that Kenya was quickly approaching independence. Constitutional conferences held between 1960 and 1963, which came to be known as the Lancaster House Conferences, progressively laid the legal foundation for an independent Kenya, beginning with reaching agreement on a majority

DOI: 10.4324/9781003648826-5

representation within government by Africans, followed by negotiations and eventual agreement on the constitutional framework of the independent state. The transition in the years leading to independence also resulted in a major reshaping of the composition of public debt. Civil unrest unsettled international investors and decreased access to London for the issuance of new debt, with access restricted since the mid-1950s. The British government played a more active role in finance, extending exchequer loans directly to the colonial government, as well as grants. This policy was in line with a broader British policy to engage more actively in the administration of colonies. Additionally, the establishment of multilateral lending institutions with the conclusion of World War II provided access to new pools of finance, which in turn began altering the composition of external debt.

The founding of the post-independent Kenyan state charted a path that was unique to the Kenyan identity, conscious of the history and societal values of the communities within the territory, while at the same time cognizant of the positive and negative attributes of the major systems of political organization that prevailed globally during that time. Upon independence, Kenya aspired to adopt a system of African Socialism that was based on incorporating the best of African traditions of political democracy.[1] African Socialism was founded upon the recognition of equal rights for each individual in society, building upon the tradition whereby an individual's voice was equal, respected and heard in society regardless of wealth or status. Equally, the system was founded on the notion of mutual social responsibility, defined as an extension of "the African family spirit to the nation" whereby individuals did the best for each other in the knowledge that cooperation in society was a prerequisite for prosperity.[2] The role of the State was to represent all citizens with impartiality and without prejudice, mirroring traditional systems that prevented any individual or group of individuals from exerting undue influence on others. African Socialism was envisioned as distinct from capitalism by preventing disproportionate influence by economically powerful groups, and different from communism by ensuring equal political rights for every citizen.[3]

Kenya faced two key structural challenges as it prepared for economic growth in a post-independent world. First, major levels of underinvestment in the education of Africans during the colonial period meant that the country faced a human capital deficit. A major effort to increase the productivity of the labor force was therefore necessary to support growth. And, second, the country had very modest national savings to leverage for development. At the household level, private savings were low due to the restricted participation that African individuals were allowed in commercial activity during the colonial period. At the public level, the World Wars were major shocks that depleted the country's public savings, and the emergency period during the Mau Mau uprising depleted the savings that had been accumulated during the post-war period. Therefore, the country faced the major challenge of closing its physical and human capital deficit without sufficient national savings. It was therefore clear that the country would need to rely on debt financing to achieve its vision of growth and prosperity. Additionally, investments in infrastructure were mostly concentrated on serving the agricultural industry in European-occupied areas, and significant infrastructure investments would be necessary to open up the rest of the country to economic activity.

Kenya's stated foreign policy was to pursue "political non-alignment" with other nations in the world, thereby allowing the country to engage fully in global trade, avoid political or ideological domination by any singular nation, expand the sources of finance available to grow the Kenyan economy and benefit from knowledge and technology from any country without precondition.[4] In practice, this foreign policy outlook meant a deliberate and conscious effort to dilute British influence by building relationships with other nations. Cognizant of the constraints to development imposed by its limited domestic savings, Kenya's foreign policy upon independence supported external borrowing from new sources of finance to overcome the immediate financial constraints to development, leveraging debt for growth while overcoming the existent structural constraints. The policy was biased towards multilateral borrowing, conscious of the possible conditionality that may arise from bilateral sources of finance. The policy stated that "… aid from abroad will not be welcomed if it is designed to promote the economic or political dominance of the aiding country. For this reason, Kenya would welcome any scheme that channeled more aid through world bodies…".[5]

The transition to independence therefore introduced a number of dynamics that transformed the composition of Kenyan debt. The structural constraints were immense. Unlike the colonial government, which leveraged the productive efforts of every individual for economic growth but concentrated public expenditure only for the benefit of a select minority, the new government was equally responsible for the welfare of every member of society. There were massive structural gaps to close in improving access to public services including education and health care for every citizen, thereby building human capital and the productive capacity of the nation as a whole, which would form the foundation for a broad-based improvement in living standards for every Kenyan. The government emphasized that the only solution to achieve the goals of African Socialism was through sustained economic growth and job creation. The nascent government was therefore committed to making significant investments in both physical and social infrastructure to address the existing structural deficits.

The government's development strategy was stated and implemented through periodic economic development plans. Kenya's first development plan placed heavy reliance on external financing, with domestic resources contributing only one-eighth of total financing. The economy continued heavy reliance on the United Kingdom to finance its immediate needs, with the majority of finance raised from both loans and grants received directly from the British government. Other sources of finance, including both bilateral and multilateral sources, remained relatively small in comparison to Britain at independence, although these sources grew in importance thereafter. The most notable bilateral sources that contributed financing in long-term loans and grants were West Germany, the United States of America and the People's Republic of China.[6] However, independence also marked a watershed moment in the country's ability to mobilize domestic capital and to develop capital markets in order to support African households and enterprises, which were able to expect more support from the post-colonial state than would ever have been possible under colonial restrictions.

With independence, Kenya also lost access to guarantees provided by the British government of newly issued debt, transitioning into a period of complete self-reliance for its debt sustainability. Access to long-term loans raised in London was lost during the emergency period, in part due to higher levels of domestic uncertainty during the emergency period caused by the Mau Mau uprising, and in part due to geopolitical events that had a significant impact on the British economy. The Suez Canal, which was opened in 1869, was nationalized by Egyptian president Gamal Abdel Nasser in 1956, displacing the consortium including France and the United Kingdom, that had run the canal for almost a century. This action precipitated the Suez Crisis, with military action by Israel, France and the United Kingdom in Egypt resulting in global diplomatic efforts and intervention by the United Nations. During the crisis, the British pound came under speculative attack that depleted the Bank of England's U.S. dollar reserves as it attempted to defend the fixed exchange rate between the sterling pound and the dollar.[7] This financial crisis contributed to tight financial conditions and higher costs in the London market, thereby restricting international access.[8] Kenya's outstanding London debt was progressively paid down over time through sinking fund contributions until the last payment was made in 1982. Access to new sources of finance also introduced borrowing in new foreign currencies that increased the share of foreign currency-denominated debt.

Following independence in December 1963, Kenya's total public debt stood at KES 1,722 million as of June 1964, of which KES 1,370 million was external debt and KES 352 million was domestic debt.[9] Almost half of Kenya's external debt consisted of funded long-term loans raised in London, which accounted for more than one-third of the total debt, in addition to unfunded debt also due to the United Kingdom's government, as well as other British contractor firms. Debt servicing for external debt amounted to KES 39 million, in comparison to the servicing of domestic debt, which totaled KES 65 million. Therefore, the relative cost of servicing domestic debt was significantly higher than that of external debt: domestic debt servicing accounted for 63 percent of total debt servicing, although domestic debt outstanding was only 20 percent of total public debt. At this point, practically all of Kenya's domestic debt was accounted for by funded long-term loans raised in East Africa.[10] Relative to the size of the economy, public debt in June 1964 was 24 percent of GDP, while debt servicing costs amounted to about 10 percent of central government revenues. The government's external financing strategy sought to secure external loans with lowest interest rates and longest tenor possible, as well as diversifying sources of external finance. Over time, the World Bank became Kenya's largest multilateral creditor (Figure 4.1). External financing was typically project-based and was dependent on the government's ability to put together bankable projects.

The years leading up to independence resulted in some major shifts in Kenya's expenditure. The advent of independence led to the

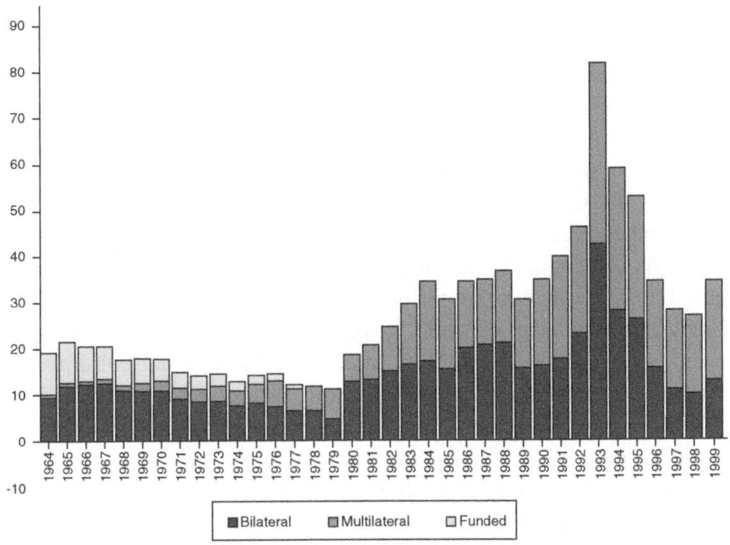

Figure 4.1 External debt by source (percent of GDP).
Source: Data from Kenya National Bureau of Statistics, Economic Surveys, 1970–2000.

departure of British expatriate public service officials, and generated significant expenditures in compensation payments, pensions and gratuities. These were for the most part met through grants provided by the British government through the Overseas Service Aid Scheme (OSAS).[11] Further, the responsibility for national defense, which was up to independence the responsibility of the British government, was passed to the national government and contributed to a large increase in expenditure to build national military capacity. Additionally, major costs were incurred with the implementation of Kenya's land resettlement program.

Agriculture in colonial Kenya was the major economic activity for both the European and African populations, contributing over 40 percent of total gross domestic product. However, the majority of investment in agriculture and supporting infrastructure was concentrated in European areas, resulting in a significant productivity gap between African and European farmers. About half of European farms were more than 1,000 acres in size and were supported through farm loans and a well-developed research program. European farms at their peak in 1961 comprised of over 3,600 holdings of land covering a total area of 7.8 million acres.[12] These farms produced the majority of Kenya's cash crop exports. In contrast, African farms were smaller and mostly limited to the production of subsistence crops. The colonial government in 1955 put into effect an intensive development plan to increase the productivity of agriculture in African areas, known as the Swynnerton Plan.[13] This plan was premised on providing farm management technical assistance, consolidating fragmented land to holdings of economic size and reorganizing the traditional system of land tenure by registering farms for title.[14]

In addition, the colonial government began discussions on a policy to begin resettlement of Africans in the rich agricultural lands restricted to European occupation, culminating in the implementation of a plan in 1962 which aimed to purchase some 1.2 million acres from European farmers for the purpose of resettlement. This plan, which came to be known as the "Million Acre Scheme", was at the time of its implementation regarded as one of the most significant land reform programs in the world, following reforms that had occurred in Latin America and the Middle East.[15] The Million Acre Scheme was both a political and economic solution that was important in easing the transition to independent Kenya. The plan was negotiated to address the grievances of displaced individuals while also providing an avenue to compensate British settlers looking to divest their assets. The scheme was financed through the combination of a loan and a grant from the British government, in addition to financing provided by the World Bank, the Commonwealth Development Corporation and the Federal Republic of Germany.[16] In 1962, a total of £1 million was spent on land repurchases, with the amount rising to £2.2 million and £4.3 million, respectively, in the subsequent two years.[17]

The implementation of Kenya's post-independence development plans resulted in significant public investment in order to develop education, healthcare and improve transportation networks, including expanding road networks and maintaining the railway network. Central to economic growth was a detailed planning process that set development objectives for each economic sector, budgeted for required spending, matched spending with identified sources of finance and tracked actual progress relative to growth targets. However, the implementation of development objectives faced the hurdle of limited skilled manpower. Aggressive increases in public investment budgets placed a strain on the public service, which faced a shortage of qualified manpower to implement development plans, despite the government's efforts to increase technical and professional training.[18] In order to ensure strong administration of projects, the government relied on expatriates to fill senior positions as educational programs were implemented to improve the quality of human capital in the country.

The overall political transition of East Africa to independence in the early 1960s also created some challenges in the external sector. Kenya, Tanzania and Uganda shared a common marketplace where trade across borders was uninhibited, and which was supported by shared institutions, including the East African Common Market and the East African Common Services Organization (EACSO). In addition, the three countries carried over the functions of the East African Currency Board (EACB) following independence. The three countries recognized the advantages offered by the larger common market, which provided advantages for each country. For example, landlocked Uganda depended on the port of Mombasa for its exports and imports, while Nairobi had established itself as the financial center from which investments to other countries occurred. Political negotiations leading up to independence intended to maintain the advantageous features of the common market beyond independence. In addition, the three countries were jointly liable for existing debt that had been originated to develop and maintain shared infrastructure.

A common feature across Kenya, Tanzania and Uganda in the early 1960s was a significant leakage of foreign exchange through unknown channels, which signified an unrecorded outflow of private capital.[19] These outflows contributed to pressure on the current account, which was offset in part by official grants and new borrowing. The underlying cause of the outflows was capital flight from the country due to the fear among the European and Asian communities, who were the significant members of the business community, of political instability after independence. This put downward pressure on economic activity that threatened to stymie private sector investment, and impeded the government's ability to mobilize resources for investment. To mitigate the problem, the government implemented exchange controls to check capital outflows,[20] and also provided incentives and guarantees to foreign and local investors.

The EACB was re-organized to play a more significant role in the monetary sector within East Africa. The seat of the EACB was moved from London to Nairobi, and the board's membership was changed to include the permanent secretaries of the respective territories. These changes improved the EACB's flexibility and operational capacity to meet the monetary needs of its membership, including performing duties that were generally more associated with the role of a central bank, thus increasing its remit significantly beyond its original mandate to issue and exchange currency. The EACB issued short-term finance to its member governments through the rediscounting of Treasury bills in order to cover short-term spending needs, but consciously limited long-term lending to governments.[21] The EACB also acted as a lender of last resort to commercial banks, by lowering its lending rate for crop financing when commercial banks faced unfavorable borrowing conditions in London. The EACB historically permitted only a small fiduciary element in its currency,[22] but substantially increased the total permissible amount for East Africa to £45 million in the 1960s, with £35 million set aside for loans to governments and the remainder for rediscounting of commercial paper used by commercial banks for crop finance.[23]

However, the EACB also faced some major constraints relative to central banks. Most obviously, it had no legal power to require minimum reserves from its membership and could not implement monetary policy to influence interest rates and money supply. Neither was it empowered to act as a full banker to its member governments, or accept deposits from them. The EACB envisioned the creation of an integrated East African money market through the creation of East African Treasury bills. However, positive sentiments regarding the common market began to wane, as Tanzania and Uganda felt that the shared market favored Kenya. The EACB's role and eventual existence came to an end with the decision made by Kenya, Tanzania and Uganda to establish three separate national central banks.[24]

A major milestone in Kenya's financial and economic development was the establishment of the Central Bank in 1966, which had a major impact on the country's ability to access external finance, as well as to develop domestic financial markets. The Central Bank was mandated to regulate the issuance of the Kenya shilling, which gradually replaced the East African shilling in circulation, in addition to maintaining a sound monetary, credit and banking system in the country that would support economic development and external sector stability. In addition, the Central Bank was appointed as the banker and financial advisor of the government, and was also authorized to act as a banker to the commercial banking sector, thereby purchasing, rediscounting or selling financial instruments on behalf of commercial banks for the purpose of financing economic activity.[25] It also had the authority to require and maintain minimum cash reserves from commercial banks in order to control private credit within the economy, as well as setting ceilings on commercial bank lending and deposits. In maintaining external sector stability, the Central Bank was mandated to manage the economy's external reserves, where it was obligated to use its best efforts to maintain reserves at an average level equal to the value of four months of imports.[26] Kenya was now able to control its own currency, and could also establish a robust domestic financial and monetary system to mobilize domestic resources for development finance through the issuance of instruments including Treasury bills and bonds.

Central to the government's policy to deepen domestic savings, and therefore finance investment, was the establishment of a social security fund. The country's demographics at independence were such that the majority of the population was young, although the dependency ratio was high due to the large number of young individuals below working age.[27] The government sought to borrow against the productive capacity of the country's youthful demography by leveraging the fact that social security contributions were expected to outstrip the payment of benefits. The National Social Security Fund (NSSF) was established in 1965 to allow individuals to save income for social security.[28] The NSSF offered a critical base for the mobilization of domestic savings, quickly becoming one of the largest domestic creditors to government, with its share rising to more than 50 percent of domestic debt within 10 years, by 1975 (Figure 4.2). By mobilizing domestic savings, Kenya envisioned becoming a net repayer of foreign loans by the early 1980s.

Commercial banks also played an important role within the capital markets. In 1968, the commercial banking space was dominated by foreign banks. There were 11 foreign banks operating in Kenya. The financial sector continued to be well integrated with the United Kingdom, with the three largest Kenyan banks having their headquarters in London. These were National and Grindlays Bank, Barclays Bank and Standard Bank. The six smaller banks had their headquarters in a mixture of locations, in India, Turkey, Pakistan and the Netherlands. The government made investments to increase the domestic ownership of the financial sector beginning in 1968. Two

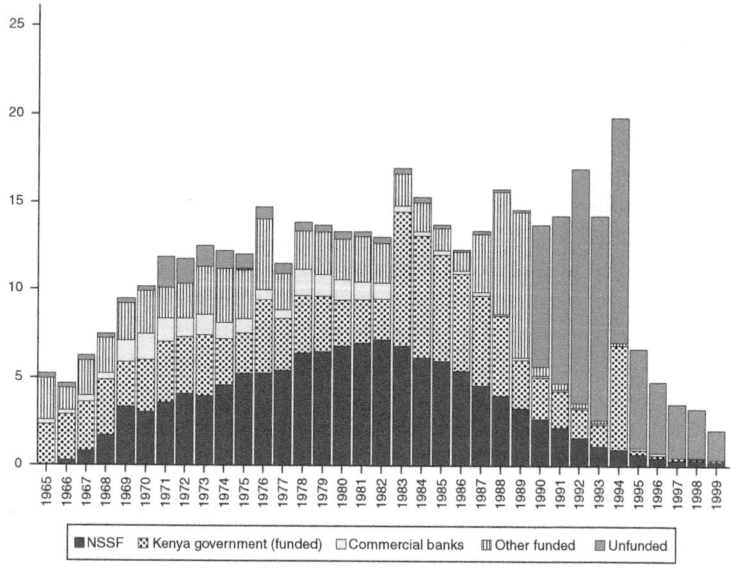

Figure 4.2 Domestic debt by holder (percent of GDP).

Source: Data from Kenya National Bureau of Statistics, Economic Surveys, 1970–2000. Kenya government funded debt includes Central Bank and Central Government, including sinking funds and pension funds.

banks were established within the year. First, the Co-operative Bank of Kenya was established in January 1968 in order to provide credit to rural cooperative societies. Next, the National Bank of Kenya was established in September 1968 as the first government-owned indigenous bank, in order to compete with the foreign banks.[29] Two years later, in 1970, the government reached an agreement with the National and Grindlays Bank to purchase a majority shareholding, and thereafter established the Kenya Commercial Bank.

In the 1970s, the government continued its efforts to mobilize domestic financial resources in order to finance its massive development needs. In particular, the government borrowed through the Central Bank and issued government paper to plug the deficit and finance its development strategy. Advancements in the domestic financial sector such as an increase in domestic bank deposits and the government's decision to acquire major stakes in the top three commercial banks further buoyed government domestic borrowing. As a consequence of these efforts, the share of domestic borrowing increased to account for half of all borrowing. The NSSF, commercial banks and insurance companies were the main domestic creditors to the government, who were encouraged to invest by the increasing rediscount rates and rates on advances on government paper. Through deliberate efforts to leverage both domestic and external financing, Kenya was therefore able to make significant progress in developing capital markets and in accessing finance for public investment in the years following independence.

Notes

1 Republic of Kenya (1965).
2 Republic of Kenya (1965), p. 4.
3 Republic of Kenya (1965).
4 Republic of Kenya (1965), p. 8.
5 Republic of Kenya (1965), p. 9.
6 Ministry of Economic Planning and Development, Economic Survey, 1967, Table 165(b), p. 140.
7 Boughton (2000).
8 IBRD (1960), p. 20.
9 Ministry of Economic Planning and Development, Economic Survey, 1970. According to the IMF, total long-term debt in Kenya amounted to £86 million as of June 1964, of which £68 million was external. In addition, there were sinking funds at a market value of £8 million. See IMF (1965), Corr 1, p. 67.
10 IMF (1965), Corr 1, p. 67.
11 Ministry of Economic Planning and Development, Economic Survey, 1965, pp. 59–60.
12 IMF (1965), p. 14.
13 IBRD (1960), p. 8.
14 IMF (1965), p. 14.
15 See Leo (1981).
16 IMF (1965), p. 3.
17 IMF (1965), p. 18.
18 IMF (1967), p. 7.
19 IMF (1967), p. 80.
20 IMF (1967), p. 12.
21 Rediscounting refers to the process where a bank or financial institution sells its short-term promissory notes to a monetary authority at a discount, in return for cash that can be used to meet short-term funding needs.

22 Fiduciary issuance refers to the issue of currency notes without the backing of gold.
23 IMF (1965), Corr 1, p. 10.
24 Kratz (1966).
25 IMF (1967), p. 40.
26 IMF (1967), p. 41.
27 The dependency ratio is the share of the sum of those under 15 years of age and 65 or older, as a percent of those aged between 15 and 64, typically considered the working-age population.
28 IMF (1969), p. 50.
29 IMF (1969), p. 42.

References

Boughton, J. M. "The Mexican Crisis: No Mountain Too High?" In *Silent Revolution, The International Monetary Fund, 1979–1989*. International Monetary Fund, 2000.

International Bank for Reconstruction and Development (IBRD). *The Economy of Kenya*. Report No. EA-109a, May 17, 1960.

International Monetary Fund. *Kenya – 1965 Article XIV Consultation*. Report No. SM/65/67. 1965.

International Monetary Fund. *Kenya – 1966 Article XIV Consultation*. Report No. SM/67/24. 1967.

International Monetary Fund. *Kenya – 1968 Article XIV Consultation*. Report No. SM/69/24. 1969.

Kratz, J. W., "The East African Currency Board." *International Monetary Fund, Staff Papers* 13, no. 2 (1966).

Leo, Christopher. "Who Benefited from the Million-Acre Scheme? Toward a Class Analysis of Kenya's Transition to Independence." *Canadian Journal of African Studies / Revue Canadienne Des Études Africaines* 15, no. 2 (1981): 201–22. https://doi.org/10.2307/484409.

Ministry of Economic Planning and Development. *Economic Surveys*, 1965–2024.

Republic of Kenya. *African Socialism and its Application to Planning in Kenya*. Sessional Paper No. 10, 1965.

5 Economic Policies

Import Substitution, Structural Adjustment, Privatization and Debt

Kenya's major infrastructure development needs required capital imports, and debt issuance was central to financing public investment. However, capital imports also contributed to imbalances in the country's external accounts. The economy experienced significant economic gains by implementing a policy of import substitution, where imports were restricted except for capital goods needed to build capacity for local production, with the intention of stimulating the growth of domestic industry and creating jobs. With the depletion of room for import substitution, the economy pivoted to export promotion, following the successful implementation of these policies particularly in Asian economies. Ambitious development plans and the development of regional and international trade resulted in the accumulation of debt, supported by returns from sustained economic growth. However, a global economic slowdown in the 1980s resulted in debt fragility not just in Kenya but also in other developing economies across the world. As a consequence, Kenya became one of the first countries to enter structural adjustment programs led by the World Bank and IMF and backed by major bilateral lenders. These programs were unsuccessful in addressing Kenya's rapidly deteriorating fiscal position, and debt restructuring was ultimately necessary to return the economy to fiscal sustainability.

Economic policy regimes in Kenya over the years following independence tracked global policy advice that reflected experimentation across evolving schools of economic thought. Development economics gained prominence in the 1950s in recognition that standard economic theory, developed within an industrialized economy context, and perhaps even with the interests of industrialized nations in mind,

DOI: 10.4324/9781003648826-6

may not necessarily apply to newly independent and developing economies across Africa, East Asia, Latin America and the Middle East. The focus of capitalist developing economies was how to increase productivity at full employment in order to improve living standards and catch up to industrialized economies, where international trade was one of the crucial elements within the policy debate. Some critical links emerged between the implementation of economic policy regimes over time and public debt. First, exchange rate and international trade policies resulted in balance of payments imbalances that in some cases precipitated crises that impacted access to debt markets and affected the repayment of foreign currency-denominated debt. Additionally, economic policy in developing countries was influenced through conditional access to concessional debt, most significantly through the structural adjustment programs implemented by multilateral organizations.

The first major economic policy strategy that Kenya implemented following independence was import substitution. When Kenya embarked on this strategy, import substitution already had a long history of implementation in developing economies, with a pattern that at first reflected promise and growth upon implementation in a number of countries, but that ultimately produced disappointing results. At the most basic level, import substitution referred to the replacement of imports of manufactured goods with equivalent domestically produced goods. Particularly, in the 1950s, import substitution became a prevalent policy in Latin American nations and received intellectual backing from some prominent figures in the blossoming world of development economics, including influential voices in the United Nations, such as Raúl Prebisch, who was the first executive secretary of the United Nations Economic Commission for Latin America (UNECLA) and the first secretary general of the United Nations Conference on Trade and Development (UNCTAD). Proponents of import substitution argued that developing countries should implement policies to discourage the importation of manufactured goods for consumption, and instead focus on building capacity to produce those goods domestically.

At the heart of import substitution was a rejection of the principle of comparative advantage, whereby it was believed that developing countries, particularly those rich in resources, would be locked in a cycle of extracting and exporting primary commodities to industrialized countries in exchange for imports of value-added goods. This cycle would thereby create a trap that developing economies would not be able to escape from, as the terms of trade, a measure of export prices relative to import prices, would continuously deteriorate for them.[1] A country with a positive terms of trade experiences a greater relative increase of export prices in comparison to import prices, indicating that a greater quantity of imports can be purchased for the same amount of exports. Advocates for import substitution believed that terms of trade would deteriorate because the prices for value-added goods would increase over time relative to those of primary commodities, thereby leaving commodity exporters at a permanent disadvantage.[2] In turn, increasingly expensive imports would consistently increase pressure on the utilization of foreign exchange. Critically, capital intensity and innovation in value-added industries would also lead to increasing disparities in the quality of human capital and innovative activity between countries specializing in the extraction and export of primary products in comparison to those innovating with primary inputs. As a consequence, import substitution policies advocated the restriction of imports to capital goods necessary to build capacity for local production, thereby increasing domestic value-addition and investment in technology, increasing opportunities for local employment in higher quality jobs, and lowering pressure on the use of foreign exchange due to lower imports.

In practice, import substitution created major inefficiencies that overshadowed its intended outcomes. Chief amongst the issues was the manner in which domestic industries were protected, either through quotas or tariffs. Frequently, elite capture and corruption occurred whereby domestic industries were protected as a means to accumulate rents that benefited select individuals. As a consequence, economic policies were not set according to any objective rationale, and inefficient firms were created that were protected from competition, but which fell far short of being capable of competing in export markets. Thus, even though import substitution policies protected inefficient domestic industries by design, they did not create incentives that improved the efficiency of domestic industry sufficiently to compete internationally, even though these protectionist policies were in theory expected to grow domestic industry and increase its contribution to overall economic growth. In fact, import substitution may have done the opposite by creating and supporting an environment that increased the inefficiency of firms by virtue of eliminating competition. Additionally, import substitution policies led to overvalued real exchange rates due to restricted imports that in turn lowered the competitiveness of exports. By the mid-1960s, there was mounting evidence of the ineffectiveness of import substitution policies, and by the end of the 1960s, these policies had fallen out of favor in intellectual economic discourse, although they have continued to be applied by governments even in modern-day economies.[3]

Despite the mounting global evidence against the effectiveness of import substitution, these policies were advocated for and implemented following Kenya's independence in order to protect the nascent domestic industrial sector, as well as to protect the country from potential foreign exchange crises arising from the need to obtain foreign currency to pay for imported goods. Following a period of stable growth in the 1960s, the government announced an ambitious plan for the 1970s that centered on the development of rural areas, infrastructure improvements across the country, and ramping up the development of local industry through investment and protection by means of continued import substitution. However, it was also recognized that the strong growth targets would require significant capital imports that would result in a higher growth rate for imports relative to exports even under the most optimistic assumptions of export growth.[4] Rather than lower investment targets, the government elected to cover the expected widening of the current account deficit with a mix of both domestic and external financing.

As a consequence of the implementation of its development plan, Kenya's industrial sector expanded and made a major contribution to the country's overall growth rate, expanding output by three and a half times between independence and 1979 and averaging an annual growth rate of 9.5 percent during this period relative to 7 percent for the overall economy. The government attributed this growth to the successful implementation of import substitution policies.[5] These policies endured until the end of the 1970s, when pressure on balance of payments spiked due to global stagflation, during which global economic growth slowed down while inflation was increasing due to increasing oil prices. At this point in time, the share of imported consumption goods had declined to below 15 percent of total imports, leaving limited room to exploit these policies further for economic growth, at a time when domestic economic growth had slowed due to external conditions. These factors prompted a shift in government policy to resource-based, export-oriented production.[6]

Kenya's overall structure of public debt evolved in the 1970s to an increase in the share of domestic debt relative to external debt, and a shift in the mix of external debt to a higher share of multilateral debt relative to bilateral debt. The economic crisis in the late 1970s illustrated the limits of both external and domestic debt financing. On the one hand, the possibility of default on external borrowing risked damaging the country's hard-earned international reputation for creditworthiness, while on the other hand, reliance on domestic finance risked generating uncontrollable inflationary pressure. The government was therefore forced to lower its overall ambitions and outlook for economic growth.[7]

Export promotion gained momentum globally as import substitution waned in intellectual popularity. Countries such as Taiwan and South Korea enjoyed economic success by focusing on policies that created incentives for exports instead of restricting imports. In Kenya, the pivot to export promotion occurred at the same time as structural adjustment policies were beginning to gain momentum in global development policy. The global experience with export substitution highlighted some key characteristics that made it more successful than import substitution. First, export-oriented countries permitted ready and competitive access to imports of capital and intermediate goods, which were critical inputs for domestic productive industries and supported their competitiveness. Second, export-oriented regimes had exchange rates that were more fairly valued than the overvalued exchange rates that characterized import substitution regimes, where import restrictions did not allow nominal exchange rates to depreciate and diminish arbitrage opportunities due to price differences in commodities between domestic and foreign markets. Lower nominal exchange rates for export-oriented regimes supported relative competitiveness and provided incentives for exports. And third, export-oriented regimes tended to have simple tariff regimes, and therefore lower bureaucracy and greater trade efficiency, that allowed exporters easier access to international markets in contrast to the heavy restrictions that characterized import substitution.[8]

Export promotion policies were understood to be more difficult to initiate and support than import substitution, particularly due to difficulty in overcoming domestic political resistance, but once initiated, were more likely to realize higher returns relative to import substitution. As exporting countries were not limited to the size of domestic markets, they could establish plants of economically efficient size to serve international markets, and therefore gain economies of scale. Additionally, these economies, by virtue of not being restricted to utilizing domestic inputs, were able to import intermediate inputs at internationally competitive prices. In terms of factor inputs, the relative abundance of unskilled labor in less-developed economies meant that these economies were more likely to specialize in the production of exports that were labor-intensive.[9] Thus, the premise of export promotion was to create domestic industries that were internationally competitive by virtue of supporting rapid integration and scaling within global markets, as opposed to import substitution, which sought to enable domestic industries to scale by virtue of protecting them from global markets.

Kenya's export promotion policy was centered on an export compensation scheme that was structured to provide incentives for exports, through risk measures such as export credit and guarantee schemes. At the same time, import quotas were replaced with tariffs, which were to be progressively lowered as domestic industry improved its productivity. However, at the outset, the export promotion strategy faced challenges given that the East African Community, a major market for Kenyan exports, had recently broken down in 1977. Further, protection of foreign markets and Kenya's relative inexperience in penetrating these markets muted initial growth expectations.

At the start of the 1980s, Kenya's economic trajectory deteriorated and veered dramatically off course due to some key domestic and external shocks. Having survived the oil price shock following the Iranian revolution in 1979, the global recession caused by the Latin American debt crisis in 1982 and domestic uncertainty due to the attempted coup in the same year left the economy in a highly fragile state. Credit to the private sector leveled off after growing steadily throughout the 1960s and 1970s. Real GDP growth slowed to an average of 3 percent between 1980 and 1985 from an average of 7 percent in the preceding period since independence.[10] Further, the overall fiscal balance deteriorated to almost 10 percent of GDP by 1982.

The problems at the beginning of the 1980s were not unique to Kenya, and the majority of African economies fared much worse. In fact, up to this point, Kenya was considered a beacon and example of development despite the challenges and shocks it had endured. A sense of growing alarm across the continent due to the faltering returns after 20 years of independence prompted a sober assessment by leaders, culminating in commitments to develop regional markets and thus achieve self-sustainability and less susceptibility to shocks in the global economy. Following a meeting of African leaders in Freetown in April 1980, the Lagos Plan of Action was adopted as a framework to achieve the continent's medium-term objectives. This plan, which was an initiative undertaken by the Organization of African Unity (OAU) in conjunction with the United Nations Economic Commission for Africa (UNECA), aimed to boost growth by promoting regional development within Africa. The biggest proposal under the plan was to develop an African common market by the year 2000, with the objective of achieving economic integration across the continent.[11]

Multilateral and bilateral development partners at this point restructured their engagement with developing economies, implementing Structural Adjustment Programs (SAPs) to address the key issues perceived to have contributed to the failure to achieve development objectives. SAP policies were imposed to address these structural issues, with development aid tied to the strict adherence and achievement of the policy goals. However, these policies were not driven purely by altruistic motives. The SAP framework was developed at the height of the Cold War, when Western Europe and the United States sought to limit the influence of the Soviet Union in Africa. Thus, the policies were also driven by the geo-political motive of consolidating the influence of the West in Africa.

Structural adjustment programs were implemented between 1980 and 1999. The two key institutions that led the implementation of SAPs were the IMF and the World Bank, with the IMF leading the macroeconomic agenda and the World Bank providing structural lending. SAPs included sectoral and structural adjustment loans. The philosophy underpinning the implementation of SAPs was to reduce poverty, shifting the focus of lending programs from infrastructure development, and prompting the development of metrics to measure and track poverty rates. There was also a recognition that policy implementation was holding back development more than access to development finance, prompting a shift in philosophy to policy reform.

The key pre-conditions for SAPs included market liberalization by freeing foreign trade and currency exchange rates from controls, implementing privatization of state-owned enterprises and reducing state intervention in economic activity.[12] Market liberalization policies were intended to eliminate the protection of inefficient domestic industries, exchange rate policies that created pressure on reserves, and subsidization of certain households such as urban consumers. Western economies, as the key trading partners of African economies, were also well positioned to benefit from market liberalization. Lower state intervention policies were intended to address high levels of corruption, excessive state control and gross resource mismanagement. These key policies were adopted as a template for multilateral development programs globally, and were codified in the influential Berg Report by the World Bank.[13]

Kenya entered its first structural adjustment loan with the World Bank in 1982, as one of the first countries to enter the program. Additionally, IMF lending to Kenya between 1982 and 1999 totaled SDR 1.05 billion in eight lending instruments, of which SDR 728 million was drawn.[14] During this period, Kenya's external debt skyrocketed. In the 1970s, the composition of Kenya's debt had dramatically changed following the successful implementation of policy measures to develop domestic debt markets and decrease the reliance on external finance: from a low of 18 percent in 1966, the contribution of domestic debt to total debt had increased to 55 percent by 1979 (Figure 5.1). However, there was a collapse of this policy and the contribution of external debt subsequently spiked.

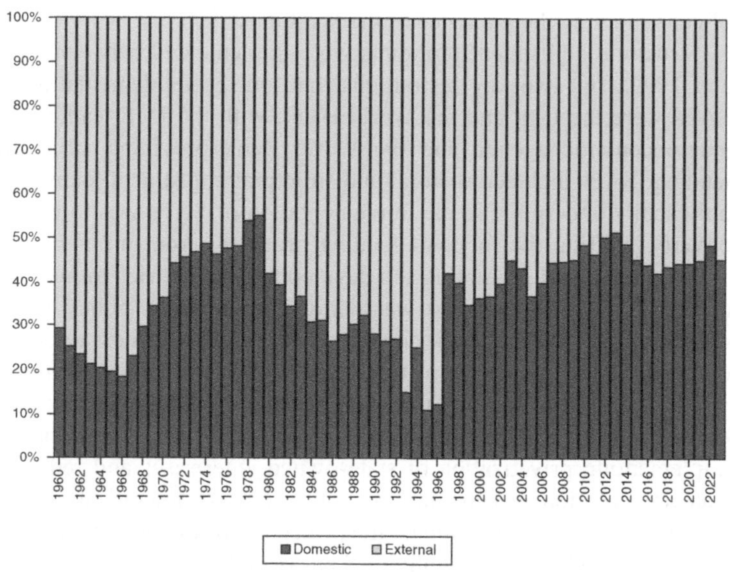

Figure 5.1 Contributions to total debt (percent).

Source: Data from Kenya National Bureau of Statistics, Economic Surveys, 1970–2024. Official statistics from 1997 onwards include short-term borrowing.

Following independence, Kenya's total debt relative to the size of the economy was relatively low and fluctuated between 20 and 30 percent of GDP from 1960 until 1979. But following the global economic turmoil in the 1980s that led to the introduction of SAPs, Kenya's total debt increased to 96 percent of GDP by 1993, with external debt comprising 81 percentage points of the total.[15] Public debt servicing increased dramatically during this period as well. From independence up to 1980, total debt servicing relative to total government revenues was relatively steady, on average 11 percent of revenues and never surpassing 15 percent of revenues. The contribution of both external and internal debt servicing was almost on par, with external debt contributing 5 percentage points and internal debt the remaining 6 percentage points. However, debt servicing increased dramatically over the next 10 years. By 1989, total debt servicing had increased to 51 percent of national government revenues. Even though external debt comprised by far the larger share of total debt, at 68 percent of total debt, domestic debt servicing payments were 32 percent of government revenues relative to 19 percent for external debt. By 1994 total debt servicing had surpassed 100 percent of government revenues, reflecting a serious economic crisis. At this point, domestic debt servicing alone was 73 percent of government revenues.

Kenya's performance during the SAP era was disappointing. Economic growth declined from an average of 4.2 percent in the 1980s to an average of 2.2 percent in the 1990s, the worst years of economic performance in Kenya's post-independence history. In the 1980s, there was a serious decline in both public and private investment, which accelerated a trend that was already underway in the 1970s. By the mid-1990s, real private investment was at a low of 5 percent of GDP, a level far below 10 percent or higher of GDP that was seen in the 1960s and 1970s.[16]

Trade liberalization in Kenya was disappointing except for some targeted successes in horticulture and apparel exports. As a consequence of SAPs, prices in Kenya were decontrolled in 1988 and interest rates were deregulated in 1991.[17] By the end of 1991, all import and export controls had been abolished except for a small list. Exchange rate controls were removed in 1993. The privatization of key parastatals during this period was slow, with only a small share of non-strategic enterprises privatized due to a combination of political resistance to give up appointments as well as difficulties in finding buyers.

Following their implementation, the performance of SAPs was universally been determined as underwhelming. Within Africa, only a handful of programs out of all SAP programs were considered successful, including Ghana and Uganda. Little economic progress was seen in Africa while debt levels remained elevated. Although the policies implemented led to major improvements in trade liberalization, governance improvements were few. SAPs have subsequently become the topic of intense debate over their merits and de-merits, with two polarized schools of thought.

Supporters of SAPs argue that the programs were economically sound, and economic performance would have been worse without them. They argue that key market liberalization policies that improved the foundation for economic growth were implemented, and in fact, that these essential reforms should have been implemented sooner. Further, they argue that the failure of the programs was due to poor monitoring of the conditions, the use of dated information, and the imposition of conditions that were too general.[18] On the contrary, SAP critics argue that the implementation was overly economic, apolitical and prescriptive. The policies were not tailored to individual economic circumstances, and the heavy-handed approach resulted in a failure for African economies to genuinely own the programs. Further, there were adverse selection issues, whereby economies that received development financing were not serious about implementing institutional reforms. In the case of Kenya, the failure of SAPs is blamed on lethargic implementation of policies, and at times the implementation of policies that were completely contrary to stated policy objectives.[19] These criticisms raise serious questions about incentives for policy reform, given the failure of domestic ownership despite the fact that national development plans and priorities across many African economies were aligned in principle with the policies advocated by SAPs.

As a consequence of poor performance in SAPs and the ever-increasing debt burden, there was increasing pressure for debt forgiveness in a number of developing economies, including Kenya. High levels of indebtedness led to the declaration by African leaders in 1987 of a common position with regard to Africa's external debt crisis.[20] The declaration urged the international community to address comprehensively the critical economic situation facing African economies as a result of the mounting debt-service burden, calling for measures that included the conversion of all past bilateral loans to grants, the suspension of external debt payments for a period of 10 years, the reduction of real interest rates on existing loans and rescheduling loans to maturities of at least 50 years.[21] Additionally, heads of state called for the removal of protectionist quota and tariff measures that restricted African exports to higher-income economies.

Given that the majority of obligations were owed to bilateral creditors and multilateral organizations, debt restructuring negotiations proceeded through official channels. The Paris Club, an informal group of official creditors that was established when a three-day meeting was convened in Paris to discuss Argentina's debt distress, became the focal point of negotiations. Today the Paris Club consists of 22 permanent members, the majority of whom are Organization for Economic Cooperation and Development (OECD) countries. The objective of the Paris Club is to find coordinated solutions for the payment of debt obligations for countries under debt distress, frequently in the form of debt rescheduling, where relief is provided by means of the postponement of payments or reducing the overall repayment obligations. Paris Club treatments are defined on a case-by-case basis, but most treatments fall under two main frameworks: the Highly Indebted Poor Countries (HIPC) initiative and the Evian approach. A country is typically invited for Paris Club negotiations after it has reached an agreement with the IMF on a program of reforms, and where the IMF's debt sustainability analysis indicates a financing gap that can only be covered with debt restructuring.

The level of Paris Club activity was low prior to the 1980s, when Mexico's default on its sovereign debt precipitated a major increase in Paris Club negotiations. During this period, agreements were simple and consisted solely of debt rescheduling at market rates on a case-by-case basis. The underlying principle guiding rescheduling was that loans were to be repaid in full, and without concession.[22] Thus, rescheduling meant only a postponement of payment obligations, but interest was capitalized and therefore increased the nominal value of the debt outstanding. Recognizing that these measures were inadequate in some cases, and that outstanding principle would likely never be repaid, the Paris Club introduced for the first time in 1988 a partial cancelation of debt, which was limited to the world's poorest and most indebted countries, in order to support debt sustainability. These terms, then known as the "Toronto" terms, canceled one-third of outstanding debt and benefited 20 countries, of which 90 percent were African. These terms were subsequently amended to raise the level of debt cancellation to 50 percent with the implementation of the "London" terms, which benefitted 23 poor countries between 1991 and 1994, and subsequently to the "Naples" terms, which raised debt cancellation on a case-by-case basis to as high as 67 percent, and also included the possibility for creditor countries to conduct debt swaps on a bilateral and voluntary basis with debtor countries, whereby the debtor country directed the servicing of debt to a fund used to finance development projects in the country. The first debt swap clause in a debt agreement was subsequently implemented in 1990.

Despite the evolution of agreement terms over the 1980s and early 1990s, the debt sustainability of some low-income economies remained extremely fragile, and by 1996, there was a broad recognition in the international financial community that the external debt sustainability of these economies, many of which were in SSA, was no longer tenable. This followed the under-performance of SAPs, which produced underwhelming growth and instead saddled additional debt upon developing economies. As a consequence, crippling debt obligations meant that these countries faced subdued growth prospects for the immediate future, even under conditions of concessional financing and the pursuit of sound economic policies. Further, the strong engagement of the IMF and the World Bank in SAPs, coupled with debt relief from bilateral lenders, meant that both the share of debt and debt service owed to these institutions also increased over time. As a matter of principle, the IMF and World Bank did not engage in any debt relief during this period due to their overriding concern to maintain preferred creditor status over all bilateral creditors and the private sector.

The preferred creditor status of multilateral institutions, supported by their lending track records, allows them to access international capital markets at low interest rates. For example, the World Bank's lending arm, the IBRD, is one of the largest issuers of debt globally, which in turn is used to finance its lending portfolio. The IBRD was established in 1944 as the World Bank's original lending arm and provides loans and guarantees to middle-income and creditworthy low-income countries.[23] The IBRD had a record of no defaults since its first loan in 1947, following World War II, until 1985. Since then, the IBRD has experienced a total of 27 default events, with the largest share of defaulted loans as a percentage of the total outstanding portfolio peaking at 4.1 percent in 1989.[24] Despite defaults on its loan portfolio, IBRD has never experienced a write-off of contractual principal or interest on any loan. However, IBRD has experienced economic loss due to delays in receiving principal and interest payments from counterparts, as it does not charge interest on overdue interest. The IBRD's operations are complemented by IDA, which was established in 1960 to support low-income economies through grants and providing low-interest loans on concessional terms.

Against the backdrop of increasingly unsustainable debt across a number of poor economies, the United Kingdom launched an initiative in 1994 to extend debt relief to multilateral debt. This proposal was initially met with an adverse reaction, but eventually gained support in September 1996, when the IMF and World Bank proposed the HIPC initiative to help eligible economies to reduce their external debt burden to sustainable levels by providing relief on multilateral debt.[25] A list of 39 countries, including Kenya, were initially considered for eligibility to HIPC. HIPC was designed to provide exceptional assistance to countries following sound economic policies in order to help them reduce their external debt burdens to sustainable levels. Unlike other initiatives, HIPC included the participation of all multilateral creditors, beyond the debt restructuring that was up to this point undertaken by official and private creditors. In order to qualify for assistance, an eligible country was required to implement adjustment and reform programs supported by the IMF and World Bank, and establish a successful track record of implementation. The country would then obtain debt relief from other existing Paris Club mechanisms, as well as other official bilateral and private creditors.

Kenya did not benefit from any of the Paris Club's major initiatives in the 1980s and 1990s, including HIPC, but benefited from bilateral restructuring of debt on a case-by-case basis, with loans from West Germany, the United States, France, Belgium and Sweden cancelled between 1989 and 1991.[26] In total, Kenya rescheduled on an ad hoc basis US$ 517 million in arrears that were outstanding in 1994. In addition, Kenya benefitted from bilateral restructuring. The reason for Kenya's avoidance of debt restructuring was to maintain the country's credit rating in financial markets, with the country instead opting to commit itself to a policy of debt reduction through the acquisition of concessional loans, encouragement of foreign direct investment, and export promotion.[27] Following this restructuring, the Kenyan government agreed to a debt restructuring in 2000 that consolidated roughly US$ 300 million of debt following successful approval of an arrangement under the IMF's Poverty Reduction and Growth Facility (PRGF). The amount included arrears of US$ 23 million, and the terms of the restructuring included an extension of loan maturities.[28] Thereafter, the Paris Club agreed with Kenya on a restructuring of US$ 350 million in 2004, becoming the first country to reschedule debt under the Evian approach.[29] This approach was tailored on a case-by-case basis for non-HIPC countries, and highly dependent on a debt sustainability analysis.

Kenya's debt restructuring in 2000 and 2004 played a significant role in lowering Kenya's external debt repayment obligations at the turn of the century, and supported the administration's policies to implement productive investments in infrastructure, that underpinned the period of economic expansion and improvement in living standards that occurred during the rest of the decade.

Notes

1 Irwin (2020).
2 Prebisch (1950).
3 Irwin (2020).
4 Government of Kenya (1969).
5 Government of Kenya (1980), p. 20.
6 Government of Kenya (1980), p. 20.
7 Government of Kenya (1980), p. 20.
8 Krueger (1985), p. 21.
9 Krueger (1985), p. 22.
10 Calculated from World Bank WDI data.
11 D'Sa (1983), p. 4.
12 Heidhues and Obare (2011).
13 World Bank (1981).
14 The SDR is an international reserve asset. The SDR is not a currency, but its value is based on a basket of five currencies—the US dollar, the euro, the Chinese renminbi, the Japanese yen, and the British pound sterling.
15 KNBS, "Economic Survey", 1995.
16 Statistics from IMF Investment and Capital Stock Database.
17 Ngeno (2000).
18 Swamy (1994).
19 Swamy (1994).
20 OAU (1987).
21 OAU (1987), p. 67.
22 Evans (1999), p. 269.

23 See The World Bank Group, "International Bank for Reconstruction and Development"; www.worldbank.org/en/who-we-are/ibrd; and World Bank Group, "What is IDA?"; https://ida.worldbank.org/en/what-is-ida.
24 IBRD (2024).
25 Gunter (2002), p. 6.
26 KNBS, "Economic Survey," 1990, pp. 77–81.
27 Ngeno (2000).
28 Paris Club (2000).
29 Paris Club (2004).

References

D'Sa, R. M. "The Lagos Plan of Action--Legal Mechanisms for Co-Operation between the Organization of African Unity and the United Nations Economic Commission for Africa." *Journal of African Law* 27, no. 1 (1983): 4–21. www.jstor.org/stable/745620.

Evans, H. "Debt Relief for the Poorest Countries: Why Did It Take So Long?" *Development Policy Review* 17 (1999): 267–79.

Government of Kenya. *Development Plan: 1970–1974*. 1969.

Government of Kenya. *Sessional Paper No. 4 of 1980*. 1980.

Gunter, B. "What's Wrong with the HIPC Initiative and What's Next?" *Development Policy Review* 20, no. 1 (2002): 5–24.

Heidhues, F. and G. Obare. "Lessons from Structural Adjustment Programmes and Their Effects in Africa." *Quarterly Journal of International Agriculture* 50, no. 1 (2011): 55–64.

International Bank for Reconstruction and Development. *IBRD Portfolio: Default Rates and Loss Given Default*. 2024.

Irwin, D. A. *The Rise and Fall of Import Substitution*. NBER Working Paper No. 27919, October 2020.

Kenya National Bureau of Statistics (KNBS). *Economic Survey*. 1990.

Kenya National Bureau of Statistics (KNBS). *Economic Survey*. 1995.

Krueger, A. *Import Substitution versus Export Promotion: What have We Learned from The Experience of Developing Countries?* International Monetary Fund, Finance & Development, June 1985.

Ngeno, N. "The External Debt Problem of Kenya." In *External Debt and Capital Flight in Sub-Saharan Africa*, eds. S. Ajayi and M. Khan. Washington, DC: International Monetary Fund, 2000.

Organization of African Unity. *African Common Position on Africa's External Debt Crisis*. 1987.

Paris Club. *The Paris Club and Kenya Agree to a Debt Restructuring*. Press Release, November 15, 2000.

Paris Club. *The Paris Club Agrees to a US$ 350 Million Debt Rescheduling for Kenya*. Press Release, January 15, 2004.

Prebisch, R. *The Economic Development of Latin America and its Principal Problems*. New York: United Nations, 1950.

Swamy, Gurushi. *Kenya: Structural Adjustment in the 1980s*. World Bank Policy Research Working Paper No. 1238, 1994.

World Bank. *Accelerated Development in Sub-Saharan Africa: An Agenda for Action*. Report No. 3358, July 1981.

6 Productivity, Employment and Public Debt

The structure of employment in Kenya changed dramatically over the years following independence. The high birth rate and young demography meant an increasing number of individuals were entering the labor force annually, but the number of formal jobs created was unable to keep up with the supply of labor. Thus, the informal economy grew over time. While the majority of jobs in the 1960s through the early 1990s were formal, the informal sector expanded to account for almost 80 percent of jobs by the 2010s. Informal employment, typically low in productivity and invisible to the authorities, had a negative impact on direct tax revenue collections, thus contributing to a financing gap that by default required debt financing to close. Further, value-for-money from the debt originated for development failed to be realized. The ultimate objective of incurring debt was to drive economic growth through productivity-enhancing investments in human capital and expansion of physical infrastructure. While the implementation of development plans initially boosted economic growth, the momentum faltered and productivity remained low, with increasingly poor governance contributing to the inability to realize gains from public investment.

The dynamics of an economy are determined by the interaction between the supply and demand for goods and services. The "real" economy includes households, firms and the government as the key domestic economic agents in a country, in addition to trade between the economy and the rest of the world. Supply is dependent on labor productivity, which is the output produced by a given worker that is in turn dependent on both capital intensity (the level of capital per worker) and technology. Total output is, therefore, determined by

DOI: 10.4324/9781003648826-7

labor productivity and employment. Across supply and demand, prices set the equilibrium level at which the exchange of goods and services occurs, thereby linking the real sector to "nominal" or monetary factors. Prices also determine levels of input for factors of production. For example, wages determine the level of labor supply by virtue of influencing the tradeoff households face between providing labor and enjoying leisure.

The link between the goods market and the money market is an important consideration in economics. Economic theory extensively discusses the extent to which monetary factors can influence temporary or permanent changes in the real sector, as well as the influence that real factors have on debt policies. The impact of monetary factors on the real economy is highly dependent on whether there are any short-term constraints or frictions that can cause prices not to adjust in the short term, instead causing the adjustments to fall on output and employment. This consideration is critical for policymaking, as it determines the extent to which "active" monetary policies can be used to influence the path of economic growth or whether the implementation of such policies instead leads to suboptimal outcomes. Under the assumption of "price stickiness", where prices do not adjust immediately, monetary variables can have real effects on output, and there is a role for active policy management. If active policies can be used to influence growth, then the use of deficit financing can be a powerful tool to influence real outcomes or to deal with economic shocks that affect demand in the short term by providing a stimulus that boosts economic growth. On the other hand, "real business cycles" explain changes in output as optimal responses to shocks to real factors (such as technology or government purchases). In this approach, there is no channel through which monetary factors can influence the real economy, and government policy interventions only serve to reduce economic welfare.

Economic theory discusses additional important channels through which public debt can impact productivity and employment. First, high levels of debt can lead to a misallocation of resources, whereby investments with short-term returns or low risk are made to maximize the ability to pay off an outstanding debt burden instead of maximizing returns to the economy. Second, high levels of debt can contribute to an environment of policy uncertainty, particularly in economies where taxation policies have a history of shifting significantly. This environment contributes to delays in longer term private investments and lowers economic growth. And third, high levels of debt can prompt governments to issue domestic debt instruments that are attractive to the financial sector and that crowd out private sector financing.

A central objective of government is to maximize the living standards of its citizens, which is in turn dependent on the economy's output per capita, as well as equity in its distribution to minimize levels of inequality. Output per capita is highly dependent on labor productivity, which can be enhanced either by improving the quality of labor, improving technology or deepening levels of capital investment. These structural issues are the major focus of government budgets and expenditure, which are targeted at improving the quality of human capital through education and healthcare systems and also improving the efficiency of production through public investments in the quality and coverage of infrastructure, for example, in roads and railway networks. Levels of domestic savings may be inadequate to satisfy the requirements for large-scale investments, and thus government policy may deliberately borrow externally in order to make productive investments.

Low productivity due to structural factors can contribute to low potential output and therefore result in a lower capacity to grow domestic savings. Kenya's labor productivity is low due to low levels of capital intensity, the quality of human capital and low total factor productivity. For example, in comparison to South Africa, Kenya's labor productivity is 75 percent lower, while its labor input is 25 percent higher. Other peer economies, including Nigeria and Ghana, also have higher levels of labor productivity than Kenya.[1] In order to boost capital intensity and raise total factor productivity, Kenya has relied on external borrowing since independence to improve the quality of education, increase the reach of healthcare services and strengthen infrastructure networks. Significant progress has been achieved, particularly in improving the quality of human capital, with major improvements in education completion rates, particularly at the primary and secondary school levels, and significant improvements in healthcare outcomes, including both child and adult mortality rates.

However, labor productivity growth has been uneven, to a large extent mirroring the effectiveness of policies across political regimes and also exhibiting sensitivity to the occurrence of shocks in the economy. This implies that the economy, rather than absorbing the impact of shocks largely through an adjustment of employment while minimizing the impact on output per worker, instead adjusts to shocks largely by lowering output per worker. Labor productivity growth increased in the 1960s but thereafter declined in the 1970s and 1980s with the occurrence of oil shocks. The 1990s saw the most serious decline in labor productivity, which turned negative in the mid-1990s, as the Kenyan economy faced its most challenging period and Kenya's public debt increased to the highest levels in its history. Following the restructuring of Kenya's debt at the turn of the century that lowered public debt levels to below 40 percent of GDP, and with investment in public infrastructure during the mid-2000s, Kenya's labor productivity growth increased rapidly. However, there has been a decline in labor productivity over the last decade that has been deepened by the impact of the COVID-19 shock in 2020.

A decomposition of economic growth sheds additional light on the drivers of growth, illustrating that the contributions of production factors have changed significantly over time. Economic growth can be decomposed into contributions by labor, capital and total factor productivity, which is a measurement of the impact of advances in technology, a broad term that includes technical advances, improvements in the quality of human capital, and other positive externalities through a myriad of factors, including efficiency-enhancing improvements in the quality of infrastructure and access to markets (Figure 6.1). The contribution of total factor productivity to growth is measured as a residual factor due to difficulties in quantifying it directly and encapsulates the sum total of a large number of factors.

The contribution of labor input to GDP growth has remained relatively stable over time, showing an increasing trend with Kenya's growing population, which fed into the country's growing working-age population as the country's young individuals reached working age. However, since the turn of the century, the contribution of labor input has been trending downwards and declined significantly during the COVID-19 pandemic. In comparison, the contributions of capital input and total factor productivity growth have shown much greater variation over time. In the immediate years after independence, the major contributing factor to GDP growth was total factor productivity growth. However, this contribution trended downwards beginning in the 1970s, turning significantly negative in the 1990s.

As a residual, the volatility of total factor productivity is unsurprising and includes a number of factors that are difficult to measure. The negative contribution in the 1990s is likely explained in part due to a decline in technology, as evidenced, for example, by

Figure 6.1 Contributions to GDP growth (percentage points, 10-year moving average).

Source: Data from The Conference Board, Total Economy Database, 2024.

underinvestment in the maintenance of public infrastructure leading to the deterioration of road and railway networks, the impact of suboptimal public investment decisions reflecting poor governance and accountability, and the postponement of private investment in plants that resulted in greater wear and tear. However, the decline in total factor productivity also likely reflects a significant underutilization of production capacity and labor. In particular, it reflects the contribution of the informal sector, where higher levels of underemployment are likely relative to the formal sector and which is more difficult to track in official statistics. The significant volatility of total factor productivity relative to labor also reflects the likelihood that firms in the formal sector prefer to maintain employment during economic cycles and instead tend to adjust to changes in demand and economic shocks by lowering hours worked and wages. Since the turn of the century, the contribution of total factor productivity has been trending upwards, although it still remains low.

In contrast, the contribution of capital increased sharply in the late 1960s, mirroring government policies that encouraged investment in industry and protected local industry through import substitution policies. However, the contribution of capital trended downwards from the late 1970s to the mid-1990s, coinciding with the period during which economic strategy shifted to the promotion of exports and supporting the growth of the informal sector. During this period, structural adjustment policies were also implemented, and political economy issues, including governance and transition of the structure of government, were central. Following the turn of the century, the contribution of capital has increased to become the major contributor to economic growth, although its contribution has leveled off in the 2010.[2]

Closely linked to productivity and the improvement of living standards is competitiveness. Competitiveness increases when productivity increases relative to costs, and hence improvements in competitiveness can be achieved through a combination of investment in skills and technology, as well as cost-cutting. Highly skilled labor is more productive but also demands higher wages. In contrast, an economy can improve its competitiveness by virtue of limiting wage increases in an economy that is labor-intensive. However, low wages limit the improvement of living standards, and economies that rely on cost-cutting and low wages are likely to find sustained competitiveness difficult to maintain due to constantly evolving efficiency-enhancing technology.

An economy's ability to grow is closely linked to its demographic dynamics. On the one hand, a young and growing population offers the potential of productive labor input, which contributes directly to growth. However, improvements in living standards require that the growth rate of economic output be higher than population growth. Therefore, countries with high population growth rates are also forced to achieve higher economic growth rates in order to improve household wealth. Further, the quality of labor, which is determined by the level of skill and experience, is a critical determinant of productivity. Demographic dynamics have historically played a central role in determining Kenya's ability to take off economically and improve its living standards. Households contribute labor and capital to productive activity, and the number of jobs created must exceed the number of individuals joining the labor force in order to ensure adequate opportunity is created. Thus, employment and economic growth are closely interlinked with demographic patterns.

Additionally, there are significant links between employment and public debt, with causality running both ways. Economies at risk of default due to high debt servicing obligations may impose austerity measures to lower debt levels that in turn depress economic growth and increase unemployment. Conversely, economies with high levels of unemployment may finance policies to lower unemployment rates by raising levels of public debt in the short term, under the expectation that improved employment and economic growth will generate tax revenues that can pay off the debt incurred. Empirically, evidence shows that economies with high levels of public debt tend to have higher levels of unemployment.[3] A further link between employment and debt is found in the structure of employment. Although significant policy efforts have been exerted in growing formal sector employment, these efforts have largely failed. Instead, the informal sector has grown over time to become the major contributor of employment to the economy, with difficulty in collecting taxes from this sector contributing to the government's financing gap.

The definition of the informal sector, also known as the "shadow" economy, is a matter of debate, but one of its generally agreed characteristics is that economic activity within the sector is either not taxed or is difficult for the government to tax. Globally, the contribution of informal sector gross domestic product is estimated at between 15 and 35 percent of total GDP, and today, some 60 percent of global employment is informal.[4] Despite its significant contribution to economic activity, the informal sector's limited contribution to government revenues means that over time a declining share of the workforce has been contributing to government revenues through personal and corporate income taxation, although revenues are still collected indirectly through consumption taxes such as value-added tax and targeted excise taxes.

High population growth rates have historically exerted pressure on the Kenyan economy's ability to improve individual welfare. At independence the population was growing rapidly at a rate of 3.2 percent, with the growth rate continuing to trend upwards. It was not until 1982, when the growth rate peaked at 3.9 percent, that it began to trend downwards and declined to a rate of 2 percent in the 2020s. Even then, the population growth rate is twice the global rate of 1 percent. The impact of high birth rates on population growth was amplified by the decline of mortality rates. Infant mortality rates were above 10 percent in 1963 and declined rapidly to 7 percent in the 1970s and 6 percent in the 1980s.[5] Additionally, life expectancy at birth increased from 49 years in 1963 to 58 years by the end of the 1980s. Thus, more people were being born and living longer. At independence, Kenya was also a very young economy where 48 percent of the population was aged 15 or below. This presented two key problems. First, the young-age dependency ratio, a measure of the share of young individuals aged below 15 to the working-age population, was very high at 99 percent in 1963, much higher than the global young-age dependency ratio of 65 percent. Therefore, as a consequence of the high birth rates, a relatively small working-age population was responsible for providing livelihoods for a large population of children. Of course, this measure does not account for the fact that a large number of children engaged in work, but it does give a clear indication of how young Kenyans were on average. Over time, the second issue was of significant concern: the large number of young individuals meant that a large and ever-increasing number of individuals was expected to join the labor force each year. Therefore, it was essential to create jobs to absorb these new entrants.

Kenya was an overwhelmingly rural country in 1963, with over 90 percent of the population living in rural areas. Rapid urbanization following independence, with large numbers moving to cities in search of opportunity, created an especially acute need to create jobs in urban areas. The impetus for migration was the large wage differential between cities and rural areas, where the majority of high-income jobs were concentrated in the growing industrial and services industries, which were concentrated in urban areas. The daunting task of creating jobs was central to policymaking. Recognizing that agriculture was the major employer and contributor to the economy's output, policies were implemented to secure land rights and increase both productivity and employment within the sector. The Million Acre scheme was the government's first major undertaking to promote job creation by creating opportunities in small-scale agriculture. Additionally, in the 1980s, the major focus of development strategy was shifted to increasing productivity in rural areas in order to decrease migration pressure.

The implementation of policies by government to increase the supply of equitable job opportunities was expected to increase the share of wage employment over time, with the ultimate objective of having wage employment account for the majority of productive opportunities in the economy. However, the level of skill within the labor force was a limiting factor. Primary school completion rates were below 50 percent in the 1970s and life expectancy was 47 years. The structure of wage employment changed significantly over time following independence. In the early 1960s agriculture contributed the major share of wage employment, but its contribution decreased rapidly while the contribution of the public sector grew from independence up to the early 1990s. The economic crisis in the 1990s resulted in a restructuring of the public sector that included large-scale retrenchment, lowering the contribution of the public sector until the mid-2000s to a level where it has remained steady to date. The private sector has maintained a steady contribution to wage employment but has never managed to become an engine of job opportunity creation.

Despite policies implemented to increase employment, labor supply outstripped demand, and the gap continued to grow over time. This was not a phenomenon unique to Kenya but also impacted a large number of developing economies. In the 1960s, conventional mainstream economist wisdom was that labor markets were best treated as self-regulating, whereby labor demand and supply were matched at a wage determined by market forces at equilibrium, and that adjustments in both skills on the supply side and productivity on the demand side would prompt necessary adjustments in skills across industries. In other words, the emphasis was on spurring growth through improving productivity and access to markets, while employment was treated as a residual that would grow in tandem with economic growth.

The International Labor Organization (ILO)[6] was heavily influenced by this prevailing doctrine. The focus of country plans was to develop strategies that promoted employment in the formal sector, and the conventional view was that individuals outside formal employment were underutilized, underproductive and underpaid, with their situation expected to last only temporarily. However, as employment demand in developing economies continued to outstrip economic growth and formal job creation, in part due to population growth and increasing urban migration, the ILO shifted its thinking and created the World Employment Programme (WEP) in 1969. The key objective of the WEP was to place job creation at the center of national planning as an explicit policy objective rather than as a consequence of success in other development efforts.

Formal recognition of the important role played by the informal sector was achieved during a visit by an ILO mission to Kenya in 1972. The term "Informal Sector", originally coined by the University of Nairobi, was adopted by the ILO in a groundbreaking report that gave an in-depth analysis of the role informal enterprises played in creating employment and that introduced research on informal enterprises onto the global scene.[7] The report placed emphasis on providing deliberate support to the informal sector, which was largely ignored, rarely supported, and, in fact, actively discouraged by the government. These key concerns have endured in the country since the ILO report was published.

After intervening in labor markets since independence, the government signaled its intention to shift its policy in the 1980s,[8] and placed a larger emphasis on supporting opportunity within the informal sector. By the end of the 1980s, there were 600,000 people employed in 350,000 small enterprises across the country.[9] Today, Kenya's informal sector employs the majority of the Kenyan labor force, contributing over 80 percent of employment. This share has grown from less than 50 percent of total employment during the early 1990s (Figure 6.2).

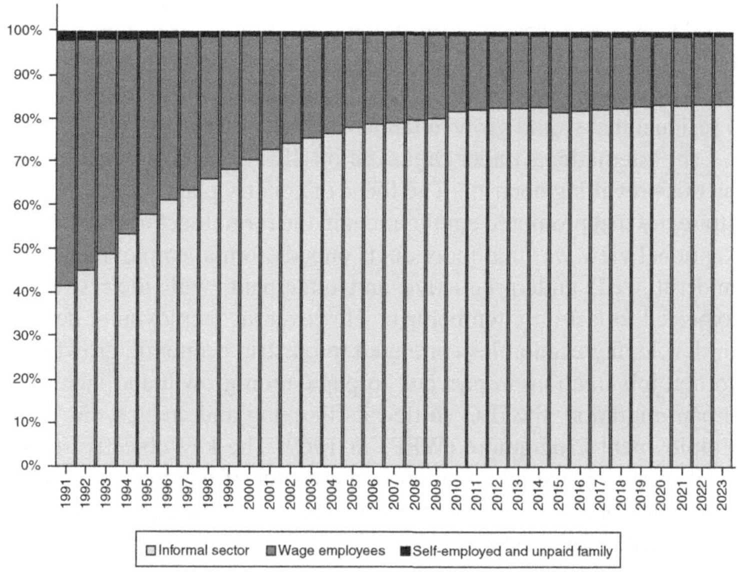

Figure 6.2 Contributions of formal and informal sector employment (percent).

Source: Data from Kenya National Bureau of Statistics, Economic Surveys, 1995–2024.

Structurally, the growth of the informal economy over time has also impacted Kenya's economic growth. Policies promoting the growth of formal employment have to a large extent failed, not only in Kenya but also to a large extent in other developing economies in Africa, Asia and Latin America.

The increase in the size of the informal economy has meant that although it has absorbed the major share of the labor force, productivity levels have remained low. The majority of informal enterprises are micro- and small enterprises engaged in low productivity activities and are also highly credit-constrained due to their lack of adequate collateral, as well as informal status. The size of the informal economy also means that a large segment of the Kenyan economy is not easily taxed and is also not well integrated into the Kenyan financial system. Due to the size of informal sector institutions as well as, in many cases, the lack of documentation, access to formal finance is limited by virtue of know-your-customer (KYC) requirements. Further, in many cases the requirements for registration with formal financial institutions are onerous and expensive for small businesses, which instead prefer to seek other avenues of finance. The under-banking of this segment of the economy, which contributes a significant share of economic output, feeds into the underdevelopment of domestic financing markets.

The shift of employment to the informal sector may in part explain the decline in the contribution of total factor productivity over time, as well as the muted growth in the contribution of capital, particularly during the 1980s and 1990s, when the informal sector grew rapidly. Overall, although investments in human capital and infrastructure, in part financed with public debt, have led to improvements in total factor productivity and Kenya's potential output, labor productivity remains low in Kenya.

Notes

1 The Conference Board, Total Economy Database.
2 Decomposition of contributions to GDP growth from the Total Economy Database.
3 See, for example, Barro, R. (1980).
4 Chacaltana and Garcia (2022).
5 World Bank WDI database.
6 The International Labor Organization is an agency within the United Nations that sets labor standards and develops policies and programs to promote decent work globally.

7 Bangasser (2000).
8 Ochieng et al. (1990), p. 353.
9 Ochieng et al. (1990), p. 303.

References

Bangasser, P. *The ILO and the Informal Sector: An Institutional History*. International Labor Organization. Employment Paper 2000/9, 2000.

Barro, R. *Federal Deficit Policy and the Effects of Public Debt Shocks*. National Bureau of Economic Research, No. w0443, 1980.

Chacaltana, J., F. Bonnett and J. Garcia. *Growth, Economic Structure and Informality*. ILO Working Paper 69, 2022.

Ochieng W. R., and R. M. Maxon. *An Economic History of Kenya*. July 1990.

7 The Impact of Domestic and External Shocks

Kenya is highly vulnerable to domestic and external shocks that have created huge short-term financing needs. The issuance of public debt is frequently desirable and necessary to overcome the sudden expenditure needs that occur due to shocks, raising finance more quickly than other alternatives. The most prevalent domestic shocks are climate-related due to adverse weather conditions, negatively impacting agricultural production that provides a major contribution to economic output and also increasing the need for social safety net spending for vulnerable households. The economy is also susceptible to global economic shocks, especially due to movements in the prices of commodities, including oil. Global economic shocks that cause a depreciation of the Kenyan shilling are especially burdensome as they increase the servicing costs of debt denominated in foreign currency. Historically, shocks that have occurred during periods when Kenya has accumulated high levels of public debt have left the country at high risk of distress. A striking property of Kenya's vulnerability is the recurrence of shocks and the limited ability of the economy to build resilience against shocks that have occurred in the past.

Shocks are sudden and unexpected events that have a negative effect on welfare. Shocks vary widely in both magnitude and duration, with more severe shocks likely to have permanent effects where an economy diverts permanently from its expected long-term growth trajectory and thereby assumes a lower growth path. Government interventions are informed by a number of factors, including the expected impact on households and contagion. Interventions frequently include an increase in expenditure, with the issuance of debt instruments one of the options to meet financing needs. The

DOI: 10.4324/9781003648826-8

issuance of debt in response to a shock is frequently necessary and efficient for several reasons. First, the magnitude of a shock may be severe enough that any existing precautionary measures prove insufficient to provide an adequate response. Second, the unanticipated nature of a shock typically creates a financing gap that must be filled quickly with emergency measures. The timelines required for other revenue mobilization measures may be too long relative to the required urgency of response. And third, the issuance of debt is likely to provide support that returns an economy more quickly to its expected growth trajectory, particularly for short-term shocks, thereby cushioning the impact of the shock and supporting the repayment of the incurred debt.

The short-term finance necessary to fill financing gaps resulting from shocks is obtained from both concessional and commercial sources. In addition, grants are frequently accessed in response to shocks, typically with the objective of supporting vulnerable households. Regardless of the source of deficit financing, economic shocks have tended to increase Kenya's overall public debt levels. Kenya is susceptible to a range of shocks due to its geography, sociocultural dynamics, economic structure and its level of integration in the global economy. The Kenyan transition from a colony to an independent market-based democracy, as well as the idiosyncrasies of its integration into both regional and international markets for trade and finance, has also exposed the economy to a multitude of other physical and economic shocks.

The major shocks that have impacted Kenya can be categorized into domestic and external shocks. The most significant domestic shocks over the course of Kenyan history relate to climate events. The persistent recurrence of poor weather conditions, coupled with their intensification over time, has resulted in severe drought episodes that increase government expenditures to support food security. In the context of climate change, and in particular the vulnerability of sub-Saharan Africa to changes in climate patterns globally, the effects of climate are a matter of major concern. In Kenya, drought occurrences in the 2010s are estimated to have cost the economy 2.8 percent of GDP per annum.[1] The magnitude of these costs surpasses any budgetary measures that can be undertaken in the short term, thereby necessitating emergency assistance through debt and grants, although it can also be argued that the inadequacy of existing resilience measures magnifies the impact of climate shocks even further. Additionally, the frequent occurrence of political shocks, particularly during election cycles, has an adverse impact on the economy.

The most significant international shocks relate to vulnerability to swings in international commodity prices, particularly fluctuations in international oil prices, where Kenya is hugely dependent on oil imports, and agricultural commodities that Kenya exports. Further, despite its limited integration in global trade and financial markets, global economic slowdowns due to shocks in financial markets in particular have had a negative impact on the economy. And finally, Kenya's exposure to global health crises has been acutely demonstrated with the occurrence of the COVID-19 pandemic.

Economic dependence on agriculture as the major engine of growth has exposed Kenya to climate-related shocks. Kenya's output has historically been heavily dependent on output from the agricultural sector, which has also been a source of employment for a large proportion of the population, particularly across lower-income segments. Following independence, significant attention was given to growing the agricultural sector with the enaction of policies to improve agricultural productivity and sustainability. In addition to supporting the supply of food crops, Kenya invested in the production of cash crops, focusing in particular on coffee, tea and horticulture exports. Rain-fed agriculture has consistently accounted for the majority of agricultural production. However, the enduring dependence on rainfall translates into an inability to secure both agricultural production and consumption against the vicissitudes of weather and therefore means that low rainfall translates into low growth and food insecurity. Poor resilience to drought episodes has heavily impacted production during climate shocks, with failed crop harvests necessitating emergency food safety net measures that have increased government deficits.

Kenya's susceptibility to periods of low rainfall is well known due to its eco-climatic conditions. Arid and semi-arid areas cover over 80 percent of the country's landmass, and only a few pockets in highland areas receive high levels of regular rainfall. The remainder of the landmass is classified as having a medium-to-high potential for rain-fed agriculture, receiving more than 700 mm of rainfall on average annually. Despite the opportunity to boost the productivity of high-potential agricultural land, the country cannot sustainably and reliably support the consumption needs of its growing population without investing in technology, including irrigation and water harvesting, to increase the area of land under cultivation.

Communities in arid and semi-arid areas have established coping techniques for periodic drought episodes. However, the recurrence of drought episodes has been intensifying over time, and the impact of each drought is compounded by the growing population—a result of the high historical birth rate and the falling mortality rate—and the fixed supply of arable land with high potential for agricultural production. Despite the well-known climactic patterns, the government has a poor track record of preparedness for climate shocks. Resilience mechanisms have included the financing of strategic grain reserves by the Cereals and Sugar Finance Corporation (CSFC) in 1981,[2] as well as the implementation of early warning systems. However, the inability to develop substantive irrigation infrastructure has meant that significant expenditure outlays are needed to respond to food security crises as they arise. Drought incidences associated with famine were recorded in 1970, 1983, 1992 and 1999 prior to the turn of the century.

Resilience to low rainfall is possible through the implementation of irrigation systems, although soil salinization is an issue of concern in some areas. Kenya is estimated to have an irrigation potential of 353,000 ha, equivalent to 3.6 percent of the total cultivable area, distributed with the greatest shares in the Lake Victoria Basin and the East Coast basin, including the Tana and Athi basins.[3] Of this total, 103,200 ha of land were under irrigation as of 2003, of which 60 percent were under sprinkler irrigation. Studies have shown the potential for both small-scale and dam-based irrigation projects.[4] However, only a small share of Kenya's potential for irrigation is currently realized. Formal irrigation began between 1901 and 1905 in Kibwezi and Makindu with the construction of the Uganda railway, and large-scale irrigation schemes were initiated in the 1950s with the development of the Mwea-Tabere, Hola and Perkerra irrigation schemes.[5] These schemes were developed using Mau detainees as free labor, with the objective of increasing agricultural land under cultivation in order to contain agitation for land by Kenyans displaced by British settlers.

The major irrigation schemes following independence were centrally managed, although small-scale schemes also developed concurrently at a slower rate. Centrally managed schemes relied on government subsidies and therefore were unsustainable. Consequently, there was a shift in policy during the late 1970s to promote a participatory model for small-scale irrigation, which prompted an increase in the area under small-scale irrigation. Irrigation was consequently led by the private sector and smallholder irrigation schemes, while the development of public schemes stagnated. However, small-scale irrigation faces some major challenges that have contributed to low rates of diffusion among small-scale holders, including the capital intensity required to install modern systems, low levels of access to finance, and misalignment of the loan products available to farmers relative to their needs.

More recently, in 2011, Kenya established the National Drought Management Authority, a specialist and permanent institution to manage drought and climate risks. Additionally, financing instruments have evolved to support the government in accessing drought relief urgently. The World Bank's Catastrophe Deferred Drawdown is a contingent financing line that provides immediate liquidity to countries to address shocks related to natural disasters. It serves as early financing as funds from other resources are mobilized and allows disbursements as soon as 48 hours after a drawdown request is made.

Other domestic shocks have played a significant role in impacting Kenya's growth and public debt obligations. In the midst of the global crisis in the early 1980s, a coup was attempted in August 1982 to overthrow the relatively nascent regime led by President Daniel Arap Moi, who became president following the death of President Kenyatta in 1978. The coup attempt demonstrated domestic political and social fragility and thereby raised uncertainty across sources of both domestic and international finance and resulted in a sharp increase in the outflow of private transfers.[6] Thereafter, in 1991, Kenya experienced a major socio-political event with the passing of a constitutional amendment legalizing a multi-party system in December, in the lead-up to the first multi-party elections in the country in 1992, which were the first to feature a direct vote for the President. The lead-up to the elections brought demonstrations and clashes across supporters of the various parties, and both bilateral and multilateral donors withheld program commitments, citing a lack of political and economic reforms. The political climate, in addition to expansionary fiscal and monetary policies by the government, contributed, among other factors, to the decline in domestic economic growth and a massive spike in domestic inflation, reaching the highest level in Kenya's history.

In addition to domestic shocks, Kenya has been vulnerable to international shocks due to its trade links with the global economy. The greatest vulnerability has been to shocks in international oil markets due to the economy's dependence on oil imports, with price shocks impacting both the balance of payments and domestic inflation. The first major international shock that impacted post-independent Kenya was the oil price shock in the early 1970s, which was sparked by a major geopolitical event: in October 1973, a coalition of Arab states led by Egypt and Syria launched a surprise attack on Israel on the Jewish holy day of Yom Kippur, sparking a war. The subsequent support that the United States and other Western allies provided to Israel prompted OPEC, a bloc of oil-rich member states, to impose embargoes on oil imports against those nations, leading to a spike in global oil prices from US$ 2.50 per barrel to US$ 9.80 per barrel and contributing to a global recession characterized by stagflation—an environment characterized by low growth and high inflation. The global oil price increase also indirectly led to the increase in prices of non-oil imports by 16 percent.[7]

The crisis found Kenya in a particularly vulnerable position, as the implementation of its aggressive development policy, which focused on high levels of public investment to improve both physical and social infrastructure, had required an increase in imports of raw materials and capital goods. As a consequence of the crisis, international reserves dropped from 6 months of import cover to 2 months of import cover and prompted the implementation of policies to cushion the economy against the impact of the shock, including the elimination of import incentives, the devaluation of the fixed Kenyan shilling exchange rate at the time by 12 percent,[8] as well as seeking short-term financing from the IMF.[9] The oil crisis had a massive pass-through to domestic prices and shifted inflation from a regime of low rates below 5 percent in the prior decade to inflation rates above 15 percent for the remainder of the decade.

Following the oil price shock in 1973, the Iranian revolution occurred in 1979, leading to the exile of the last Iranian monarch and the transition of Iran from a monarchy to a theocracy. The revolution sparked strikes that impacted Iran's oil fields, with oil production dropping by 4.8 million barrels by January 1979, equivalent at the time to 7 percent of global oil production. As a consequence, global oil prices increased rapidly despite efforts by other producers to cover the gap in volume. Between mid-1979 and mid-1980, the price per barrel rose by more than 160 percent, from US$ 13 to US$ 34. The risk of contagion drove oil prices even higher. Concerned that political crises in the region would escalate with the spread of religious fundamentalism, oil-importing economies increased their oil purchases not only to cover current demand but also to increase strategic reserves. As a consequence, panic buying played a significant role in contributing to the skyrocketing of oil prices.[10] The increase in oil prices in turn exerted significant pressure on Kenya's balance of payments. The growing fiscal deficits, incurred due to Kenya's increasing public investment over the decade, left the economy vulnerable to the oil shocks. As a consequence, economic activity slowed sharply during the year.

Western economies responded to the high oil prices in 1979 by tightening monetary policy to curb inflationary pressure. These policies sparked an increase in global interest rates that slowed global growth and resulted in a collapse of commodity prices that adversely impacted Latin American economies. These economies had taken advantage of low rates from international banks to finance the development of ambitious infrastructure projects and were dependent on commodity exports to service the payments on their external debt. The composition of external debt markets in Latin America stood in contrast to debt markets in sub-Saharan Africa. While commercial debt markets in Latin America were well developed, the composition of debt in Africa was on average more skewed toward bilateral and multilateral debt.

In 1982, Mexico defaulted on its external debt and sparked a crisis in international financial markets. Mexico had enjoyed a rapid expansion in economic growth on the back of significant oil reserves. A disclosure by Petróleos Mexicanos (Pemex), the state-owned oil monopoly, in 1977 indicated oil stocks of 60–100 billion barrels in reserves, placing Mexico's oil reserves among the top four worldwide.[11] On the back of the future revenues expected from the exploitation of these significant reserves, Mexico embarked on an aggressive public investment program, no longer viewing balance of payments constraints as an impediment to growth. In order to finance investment, Mexico tapped international financial markets, rapidly growing the share of commercial debt. In addition, the high oil prices at the end of the 1970s added color to the already rosy expected future prospects.

However, in the first half of 1981, a sharp increase in short-term interest rates within the United States and other major economies cooled global demand for oil and led to a downward slide in oil prices. Mexico's high debt exposure, and in particular a large lump of repayments that loomed in August 1982, precipitated a global crisis due to the large exposure that financial institutions in the United States,

Japan and Europe had to Mexican debt.[12] Initially, the debt troubles in Latin American countries were treated as a liquidity problem rather than a solvency problem. As a consequence, renegotiations focused on re-profiling debt repayments while maintaining the face value of outstanding debt. This was followed by the Baker Plan, which again did not support debt reduction but emphasized long-term structural reforms rather than short-term adjustment and called for the infusion of fresh capital to eligible counties.[13] These measures still proved insufficient to improve growth prospects and improve debt sustainability by the end of the decade, although they provided a window for commercial banks to lower their exposure to Latin America and to rebuild their buffers.

Consequently, the United States implemented the Brady Plan in 1989, named after the then Treasury Secretary Nicholas Brady. This plan was structured to provide debt relief for heavily indebted emerging markets. The Brady Plan included the exchange of existing debt into new obligations, Brady bonds, with an upfront payment of a percentage of the original debt. The participation of the private sector in this program was induced by a number of credit enhancements. First, principal repayments of Brady bonds were collateralized by zero-coupon US Treasury securities. Additionally, rolling interest rate guarantees were provided through funds held in trust at the Federal Reserve. The liquidity of Brady bonds was also enhanced, as they enabled commercial banks to convert their illiquid loans into tradable securities and also facilitated the participation of new institutions. The Brady plan was also tied to the implementation of IMF programs in order to promote economic reforms.

The first Brady restructuring occurred in February 1990 with Mexico, which restructured US$ 54 billion in debt, equivalent to almost 19 percent of GDP, at a discount of 13 percent. This restructuring was followed by other restructurings in Latin America, the most significant of which were in Brazil and Argentina, which restructured US$ 43 billion and US$ 28 billion in debt, respectively. Other countries with outstanding commercial debt globally also participated in Brady restructurings. Within SSA, Nigeria restructured US$ 5.9 billion of debt in 1991 at a discount of 35 percent, while Cote d'Ivoire restructured 6.5 billion of debt in 1998 at a discount of 60 percent.[14] An analysis of the Brady Plan indicates that the debt relief was important in stimulating economic recovery. Following the first Brady restructuring in 1990, Brady countries experienced sharp declines in external debt burdens and a significant increase both in productivity and output, the impact of which was many times greater than the initial value of the reductions. In essence, the impact indicated the presence of a "Brady multiplier".

Due to the Mexican crisis, the prominence of debt swaps grew as instruments to restructure distressed debt. In particular, the market for debt-equity swaps, refinancing instruments where a debtholder gets an equity position in exchange for the cancellation of debt, developed significantly in the 1980s, although there were isolated instances of the implementation of similar swaps in the 1960s. For example, in 1962, Brazil allowed the conversion of external debt into equity investments at face value and at the official exchange rate. The first debt-equity swap issuance during the Mexican Crisis occurred in 1983, when, as part of a major rescheduling package, Brazil required private borrowers to deposit local currency equivalent amounts of foreign currency borrowings in the central bank when payments became due. Some creditors decided to reinvest those deposits in the local economy, while others sold their loans to institutions planning to invest in Brazil. In this manner, the market for debt-equity swaps was established, and between 1983 and 1987, almost US$ 2 billion of Brazil's external debt was converted into equity.[15]

Debt-equity swaps subsequently grew to billions of dollars due to the Brady Plan, peaking at US$ 27 billion in 1990, with the issuance of debt-equity swaps by a large number of other countries, including Argentina, Chile, Mexico and the Philippines.[16] The basic structure of a debt-equity included the sale by a bank of an outstanding loan extended to a public sector agency under distress at a discount. The purchaser of the debt would in turn present the loan to the central bank of the indebted country, which would redeem the face value of the loan in domestic currency at the prevailing market exchange rate. The purchaser would then invest the proceeds in domestic equity, thus ultimately enjoying investment at favorable terms.

The growth of debt swap markets also prompted the creation of innovative debt swaps for development. As a consequence of the major economic instability and the high global debt burden across developing economies in the 1980s, non-governmental organizations sought innovative solutions to provide aid to developing economies while minimizing their contribution to debt overhang. An opportunity arose to provide relief while continuing development assistance through the implementation of these swaps. Debt-for-development or debt-for-nature swaps required a number of conditions to make sense. First was the likelihood that a given creditor was unlikely to redeem full payment on outstanding debt due to ongoing debt distress by the debtor nation. This condition most obviously manifested itself in debt trading at a large discount on secondary markets. In this case, the creditor weighed the relative advantage of recouping some of its outstanding debt (in addition to other positives such as reputational benefits from channeling funds to agreed-upon initiatives) against continuing to face the risk of even lower eventual payments. Second was the currency of outstanding debt, which continued to increase the repayment burden of the debtor in an environment of rapidly depreciating domestic currency.

Swap instruments allowed NGOs to purchase debt at a discount and use resultant savings in local currency to implement a range of projects spanning development and conservation. In addition to traded debt, the Paris Club implemented a framework to enable willing creditors to engage in the creation of swaps. As the debt was not traded, the terms agreed upon for swaps were dependent on bilateral negotiations. The framework for conversion of non-concessional debt was established in 1990, initially allowing 10 percent of debt to be converted, although the terms increased in subsequent years. In comparison to debt-equity swaps, the implementation of debt-for-nature swaps was much smaller. Between 1987 and 1994, only US$ 178 million of developing economy debt globally was eliminated through swaps that provided funds for nature conservation. The first African economies to implement debt-for-nature swaps were Madagascar and Zambia in 1989, respectively converting debt with face values of US$ 2.1 million and US$ 2.3 million through transactions with the World Wildlife Fund.[17] Other African economies that implemented swaps for nature in the 1990s included Ghana and Nigeria. Additionally, swaps were implemented to fund development projects in local currency, cancelling about US$ 1 billion of foreign debt by 1994.[18] Development swaps took a more holistic approach and financed diverse projects in sectors including education, health and water and sanitation. African economies, including Sudan, Madagascar and Senegal, implemented debt-for-development swaps.[19]

The global economic slowdown due to the increase in US interest rates and the consequent Mexican Crisis resonated globally and precipitated widespread debt distress in developing economies, including countries within SSA. Due to the different composition of debt in SSA, where commercial claims were limited and most debt was owed to bilateral and multilateral partners, the structure of debt renegotiations was different. In SSA, a major component of debt renegotiations involved discussions with Paris Club creditors as well as the implementation of IMF economic recovery programs, to which the terms of Paris Club negotiations were generally tied. However, similar to Latin America, debt distress episodes in Africa were first treated as liquidity rather than solvency issues, and reductions in the face value of debt did not occur initially. The prevailing economic conditions made it difficult for economies to implement their economic development plans. Kenya, like the majority of African economies, was severely impacted by the crisis and the subsequent economic slowdown that occurred in the 1980s and the subsequent sequence of debt renegotiations and economic adjustment programs that followed. Rapid currency depreciation contributed to an increasing external debt burden, and subsequent deficit monetization led to higher domestic inflation and culminated in debt distress in the early 1990s. As a consequence of external shocks, Kenya also had limited success in implementing its exports-focused industrial strategy due to the weakness of regional and global trading partners.[20]

In addition to oil supply shocks, Kenya has been susceptible to global price shocks in coffee and tea markets, where the volatility of prices in global commodity markets has provided both windfall gains and significant losses. In the late 1970s in particular, global developments in these markets impacted Kenya's economic prospects. Following a devastating frost in Brazil's southern coffee belt, hundreds of millions of coffee trees, accounting for 75 percent of Brazil's crop, were damaged, thereby precipitating a shortage in coffee from a country that contributed one-third of global coffee exports. Other major coffee producers also had supply disruptions, with too much rainfall in Colombia disrupting its production.[21] The resulting supply shock more than tripled global coffee prices and led to windfall gains for coffee producers in Kenya. However, the following year, the one-off gains were reversed as coffee production increased globally.

More recently, increasing globalization due to trade and integration of financial markets has increased global contagion due to financial sector shocks. In late 1997, the East Asian financial crisis had a severe impact on a number of countries that had for years been admired for their rapid growth and achievement in improving their citizens' standards of living. The limited integration of African financial markets, except for South Africa, to global financial markets meant the impact of the crisis was muted for most economies. Thus, African economies were insulated from contagion effects that sparked large capital outflows with the loss of investor confidence. However, the 2008 global financial crisis had a significant impact on African economies, including Kenya, due to the slowdown of the global economy, which depressed global demand and also lowered remittances. Similar effects have been observed with the 2020 COVID-19 pandemic, which also led to a major slowdown of the global economy.

Regional shocks have also had a significant impact on Kenya's economic development. In 1977, a major regional shock was experienced with the break-up of the East African Community, which was once regarded as a model for African regional integration. The lead-up to the dissolution of the community was marked with increasing tension among the member economies, with the East African Authority, which consisted of the presidents of the three nations, not meeting since 1971 due to President Nyerere's refusal to meet with President Amin. Some key ideological differences also negatively impacted trade relations. Tanzania's policy of socialism and self-reliance led to the implementation of policies that increasingly brought the economy under state ownership and control, in contrast to Kenya's emphasis on a private sector-driven economy. Additionally, differing rates of development across the three member countries created strain and resentment as Kenya obtained the greatest benefits from the regional integration, and attempts to distribute gains more evenly were unsuccessful. In February 1977, Tanzania closed its border with Kenya and effectively eliminated all trade between the two members, effectively ending the common market.[22]

The breakup of the East African Community necessitated an increase in fiscal expenditure to create Kenyan replacements of former regional corporations, as well as defense expenditure to bolster the country's security. Additionally, the break-up negatively impacted Kenya's major market for manufactured products, although overall growth was cushioned by the boom in world prices for coffee and tea that occurred in 1977.

The cyclical occurrence of domestic and external shocks, as well as the striking similarity in the impact of shocks in increasing debt fragility across economies in SSA, makes management of the risk from shocks a central imperative for government. Debt accumulation contributes to magnifying the impact of shocks on the economy, but shocks themselves lead to rapid debt increases due to foreign-currency exposure, even in instances where governments may be striving to implement prudent fiscal policies.

Notes

1 Republic of Kenya (2015), p. 5.
2 IMF (1985).
3 FAO (2005).
4 You et al. (2014).
5 Ngigi (2000).
6 IMF (1984), p. 62.
7 IMF (1974), p. 4.
8 IMF (1978), p. 2.
9 IMF (1976), p. 1.
10 Gross (2019).
11 See Bizarro (1981); Riding, Alan, "Mexico Oil Reserve Soars; Put at 60 Billion Barrels," *New York Times*, February 18, 1977.
12 Boughton (2000).
13 Shenai and Bolhuis (2023).
14 Shenai and Bolhuis (2023), p. 10.
15 Blackwell and Nocera (1988).
16 Kaiser and Lambert (1996), p. 9.
17 Kaiser and Lambert (1996), p. 10.
18 Kaiser and Lambert (1996), p. 12.
19 Kaiser and Lambert (1996), p. 13.
20 IMF (1983), p. 2.
21 See Stephen Lynton, "Taking a Coffee Brake," *Washington Post*, January 9, 1977; and Nancy Ross, "Big Rise Predicted in Coffee Prices," *Washington Post*, January 15, 1986.
22 Eken (1979).

References

Bizzarro, S. "Mexico's Oil Boom." *Current History* 80 no. 463 (1981): 49–52.

Blackwell, M., and S. Nocera. *Debt/Equity Swaps*. International Monetary Fund, Working Paper No. 88/15, 1988.

Boughton, J. M. "The Mexican Crisis: No Mountain Too High?" In *Silent Revolution, The International Monetary Fund, 1979-1989*. International Monetary Fund, 2000.

Boughton, J. M. "Northwest of Suez: The 1956 Crisis and the IMF." *IMF Staff Papers* 48, no. 3 (2002).

Eken, S. "Breakup of the East African Community." *Finance and Development* 16, no. 4 (1979).

Food and Agriculture Organization. *Irrigation in Africa in Figures: AQUASTAT Survey – 2005*. FAO, 2005.

Gross, S. *What Iran's 1979 Revolution Meant for US and Global Oil Markets*. Brookings Institution Report, 2019.

International Monetary Fund. *Kenya – 1974 Article XIV Consultation*. Report No. SM/74/219. 1974.

International Monetary Fund. *Kenya – 1976 Article XIV Consultation*. Report No. SM/76/31. 1976.

International Monetary Fund. *Kenya – 1978 Article XIV Consultation*. Report No. SM/78/76. 1978.

International Monetary Fund. *Kenya – 1983 Article XIV Consultation*. Report No. SM/83/24. 1983.

International Monetary Fund. *Kenya – 1984 Article IV Consultation*. Report No. SM/84/79. 1984.

International Monetary Fund. *Kenya – 1985 Article IV Consultation*. Report No. SM/85/260. 1985.

Kaiser, J., and A. Lambert. *Debt Swaps for Sustainable Development: A Practical Guide for NGOs*. International Union for Conservation of Nature and Natural Resources/EURODAD, 1996.

Ngigi, S. *Review of Irrigation Development in Kenya*. Working Paper, Department of Agricultural Engineering, University of Nairobi, 2000.

Republic of Kenya. *Common Programme Framework for Ending Drought Emergencies*. April 2015.

Shenai, N., and M. Bolhuis. *How the Brady Plan Delivered on Debt Relief: Lessons and Implications*. International Monetary Fund, Working Paper No. 23/258, 2023.

You, L., H. Xie, U. Wood-Sichra, Z. Guo and L. Wang. "Irrigation Potential and Investment Return in Kenya." *Food Policy* 47 (2014): 34–45.

8 Political Economy, Devolution and Debt

The relationship between the political economy and debt is multifaceted. Public debt, in particular, is an instrument that is used to exert influence on the dynamics of power across the world. In Africa, there is a long history of concessional bilateral and multilateral lending tied to the implementation of competing political ideals, a practice that is still commonplace today. Additionally, international financial markets pay keen attention to political dynamics, penalizing countries with weak institutions—particularly with regard to the protection of property rights—with higher interest rates. However, international financial markets also ironically provide disincentives for good governance, particularly where external finance comprises the major share of total finance. In these countries the government is less dependent on domestic markets, and consequently government accountability to its citizens erodes. Countries with high existing levels of debt but weak institutions find it difficult to avoid misappropriation and frequently suffer massive direct costs as a consequence, in addition to indirect costs from social projects that are either not implemented or are poorly implemented at best. In response to debt crises, such countries are also more likely to impose revenue-raising measures that exert an even higher burden on citizens rather than impose expenditure cuts and controls on inefficient spending, as such cuts also deplete opportunities for misappropriation. Such measures, when imposed on households that have already suffered large losses in living standards during an economic crisis, significantly raise the likelihood of civil unrest. From a creditor perspective, there are also risks to external debt, as there is no universal and enforceable legal framework governing the repayment of claims amongst sovereigns.

DOI: 10.4324/9781003648826-9

Therefore, other political economy considerations, including influence in global trade markets to impose penalties such as sanctions on trade or the ability to seize foreign assets or exclude a country from access to financial markets, are tools that create costs to deter opportunistic sovereign defaults.

At its core, democracy is a political system founded on safeguarding the rights of each citizen. In theory, then, highly democratic economies should also have higher protection of individual rights. Democratic rights extend to public debt, where governments must act in the best interest of citizens, given that debt is a liability to every current and future citizen. However, the common and joint accountability of the public relative to the narrow level of control exerted by a small share of individuals controlling the origination of public liabilities creates avenues for misappropriation. Elite capture occurs when individuals are unable to hold leadership accountable through the judicial system, enabling an elite minority to divert originated debt for personal gain while saddling the rest of the population with future liabilities. In an attempt to improve accountability, a large number of nations have decentralized democracy, shifting the control of investment, revenue raising and debt origination in varying measures from the national to the regional level. Evidence indicates that improvements in accountability are far from guaranteed. Further, if there is a significant gap between expenditure responsibilities and revenue generation, such that regional expenditures outstrip revenues and are highly dependent on transfers from the central government, then regional governments face incentives to overspend, resulting in overall public debt levels that are higher than optimal. In this chapter, we explore these varied and interconnected relationships in more detail.

The relationship between debt and the political economy is strongly tied to the quality of governance. Countries with strong institutions are able to borrow more and to borrow at lower rates. They are therefore able to maintain higher levels of gross debt. Japan and the United States, for example, have substantial non-resident holdings of debt despite public debt levels that exceed 100 percent of GDP, in part due to confidence in their public institutions. Conversely, countries with weak institutions find it difficult to access financing when gross debt levels begin to accumulate and struggle to make payments when borrowed funds are channeled for private benefit instead of public good.

Upon independence, the Kenyan government was organized on the ideal of African Socialism, which sought to draw upon the best of African traditions, holding social equality, dignity and justice as its foundation, while adapting to capitalism in order to spur economic development. The concept of African Socialism was in some respects similar to social democracy, frequently considered a middle practical course between capitalism and socialism, where a delicate balance was needed to create efficiently functioning markets while at the same time ensuring equitable wealth distribution. The global experience is that social democracy is difficult to achieve within capitalist societies. This model is most closely exemplified by Nordic nations, where a strong role is played by government in redistributing wealth to poorer households by virtue of social programs and subsidized public services, including education and healthcare.

Politics can be described as the struggle for power. Autocracies consolidate power within a small elite, while democracies are founded on the belief that everyone should have an equal say in decisions that affect them. Democracies protect individual rights through the election of leadership under a system of one individual–one vote, holding leaders accountable through the ballot. While many democracies are capitalist, there is no fundamental and direct relationship between the two. In fact, one can strongly argue that capitalism is in many respects directly opposed to democracy. By allowing private ownership of the means of production for profit and rewarding those in society with a greater accumulation of assets, capitalist societies allow wealthy individuals to exert a disproportionate level of influence on policy. In the United States, public policies have historically been shown to be highly responsive to the wishes of those at the top of the income distribution but not responsive to those in the lower 80 percent of the population.[1] Further, capitalism creates inequality. Evidence shows that inequality has been consistently increasing in capitalist societies over time, including in countries that have strong redistribution policies. Thus, the link between democracy and accountability is tenuous on many levels, and a strong positive link between the two is not guaranteed. Kenya has moved progressively in the spectrum of democracy, moving from a one-party state to a multi-party state and then subsequently to a devolved government in an attempt to improve governance, with mixed results.

The international political economy has played a pivotal role in influencing political organization in developing economies. In particular, the Cold War, which dominated global politics until the fall of the Soviet Union at the end of 1991, was central to international policy within sub-Saharan Africa. American foreign policy between 1947 and 1988, when the ideological struggle between the United States' brand of capitalism and Soviet communism dominated world politics, was centered around the containment of communism.[2] Africa was perceived as an unstable region ripe for Soviet ideological expansion, a view that persisted long after the end of colonialism. Thus, Western economies focused on maintaining control over sub-Saharan Africa to curb the expansion of communism.

The national interest of the United States, which serves primarily to promote American national security, has traditionally been the major determinant of American foreign policy toward other regions of the world. American and Western European interests were aligned in promoting the development of capitalism, and, in turn, these objectives influenced policy interactions with newly independent nations. The American doctrine of promoting multi-party democracy, free markets and private enterprise extended to its foreign policy, which also benefitted Western European allies that were both the major trading partners of the United States and African economies. In pursuit of the containment of communism, the United States often overlooked authoritarian regimes, corruption or economic mismanagement.

Kenya's foreign policy during the Cold War was based on the principle of non-alignment, where the country refused to take sides or be dragged into the conflict between rival groups and power blocs. Instead, Kenya promoted its own policy of African socialism. This policy was difficult to achieve in practice given Kenya's historical ties with the United Kingdom and the major influence this relationship played both in trade and finance. Further, actions such as the establishment of a United States military base in Mombasa in 1980 were also viewed globally as pro-American and opened a significant flow of resources from Western economies to Kenya.

The Cold War also played a significant part in determining access to finance within Africa by attracting bilateral aid that was tied to supporting ideological partners during the war. In comparison to other countries, the United States had an outsized influence on policy in Kenya relative to its direct contributions to external financing. The United States was a major lending partner to Kenya in the 1970s, increasing its influence and filling the external financing gap as the contribution of lending by the United Kingdom declined, and its contributions continued into the 1980s. However, Japan began seeking closer bilateral ties with Kenya in the 1980s, and its lending increased steadily to the point that by the 1990s, it was Kenya's major bilateral lending partner. Japan's foreign policy was driven by two key principles: ensuring its own security and prosperity by contributing to a stable and peaceful world, and securing natural resources through trade with newly developing economies.

Structural adjustment programs (SAPs) in the 1980s were employed as a tool to promote the implementation of capitalist policies. Although SAPs were implemented under the leadership of the IMF and World Bank, the programs were frequently structured under the insistence of bilateral donors. Further, the policies themselves were heavily influenced by the membership of the two institutions, which was dominated by the United States and Western Europe. The failure of SAPs to have a development impact may very well be attributed to misaligned political economy incentives. On the one hand, addressing the actual needs of developing economies was only primary to the extent that it coincided with geopolitical objectives. On the other hand, privileged public servants in positions to extract rents from governance failures would have had little incentive to carry out serious reforms, and the privatization and policy reform agenda would have meant losses for this group of individuals by strengthening accountability. A review of the performance of SAPs notes that failure occurred partly because "the commitment to the stated policy changes was limited to a small coterie of top civil servants".[3]

Following independence in 1963, Kenya had a long period between 1969 and 1982 as a de facto single-party state following the banning of the Kenya People's Union and thereafter became a de jure one-party state in 1982 with the amendment of the constitution. The one-party regime promoted a narrow set of incentives where party loyalty was rewarded rather than public service, and, as a consequence, levels of governance deteriorated. Further, the one-party state promoted the rise of tribal politics, where power was consolidated within certain ethnic groups, which led to the channeling of resources to develop certain parts of the country, while other parts of the country languished due to a lack of funding. Officially, single-party politics lasted only a decade, as pressure from development partners prompted a change in policy with the first multi-party elections held in 1992. Following multi-party elections, tribal politics continued to play a major role by creating voting blocs based on ethnicity. Consequently, leaders that were able to rally ethnic groups behind them began to exert an outsized level of influence.

Leading up to the multi-party elections in 1992, Kenya experienced its worst economic crisis since independence. There were multiple contributing factors, including unsettled political and social conditions that impacted the effectiveness of policymaking. Further, major economic reversals to publicly stated objectives, including the liberalization of the external sector, undermined public confidence in the government's economic management. However, the major contributing issue was gross mismanagement of the public and financial sectors, which created a financial crisis that escalated into the biggest economic crisis to date.

The financial crisis was enabled by state capture of the Central Bank of Kenya, through which several politically connected commercial banks were able to access credit irregularly. These methods included large overdrafts with the central bank, selling foreign exchange to the Central Bank with late delivery or no delivery at all, and persistent deficiencies in meeting statutory cash ratios. By March 1993, the total credit extended by the Central Bank amounted to KES 18 billion (71 percent of reserve money). Further, at this time public enterprises were in arrears to the National Treasury to the tune of KES 15 billion, of which KES 4 billion was attributable to Kenya Posts and Telecommunications alone, despite the fact that the state-owned enterprise had at the same time lent a large amount to a relatively small bank on a long-term basis.[4]

These events culminated in major economic distress, and in early 1993, Kenya incurred external payments arrears for the first time in its history, signaling high levels of sovereign stress. By March 1993, arrears had reached US$ 652 million, and the economy was in crisis with severe shortages of foreign exchange and businesses shutting down. Domestic inflation rose to 46 percent, and for the first time in post-independent history, the economy contracted by 0.8 percent in 1992. With few alternatives on the table, Kenya entered an IMF program to weather the economic storm and restore confidence in the economy. As a consequence, public debt increased to 82 percent of GDP, of which 52 percent was bilateral and 48 percent was multilateral. The two largest creditors were the World Bank and Japan, whose shares were 31 percent and 13 percent of GDP respectively. Further, public debt servicing skyrocketed to 75 percent of GDP in 1993.

There was renewed momentum in restructuring and privatizing state-owned enterprises, enforcing discipline in the management of public finances and taking actions to deter the recurrence of financial irregularities. Civil service reform was advanced with a net reduction of staff by 12,500 (5 percent of the workforce).[5] Progress was muted by an uncertain economic environment and enduring ethnic tensions between leadership and opposition parties. Further, there were important setbacks in the liberalization of the maize sector. A ban was temporarily imposed on the importation of maize and sugar, and the National Cereals and Produce Board (NCPB) continued massive purchases of maize at a price substantially above the market price. Kenya's first three-year Enhanced Structural Adjustment Facility (ESAF) expired without review due to the authorities' failure to address outstanding structural reforms. The key issues related principally to corruption and governance, including enforcing accountability with respect to financial irregularities relating to gold and diamond export compensation payments, establishing an anti-corruption authority with a strong mandate and authority to pursue corruption cases, and safeguarding the independence of public revenue collection.[6]

The implementation of reform measures continued at a slow pace until the general elections in 2002. With new government commitments, a Poverty Reduction and Growth Facility (PGRF) was negotiated with the IMF in August 2000, but no reviews were completed either. The elections resulted in a change of leadership, under which the PGRF was cancelled and a new program requested. Under the new coalition leadership, economic growth stabilized, and efforts turned to implementing a new constitution.

Political economy considerations play an important role in influencing the likelihood of default, as well as influencing the relative seniority of different classes of creditors. Sovereign debt contracts differ from private contracts in one critical respect: there is no enforceable international solvency regime, and there are no explicit mechanisms to enforce adherence to sovereign contracts. In contrast, private contracts are governed by a clear legal framework that delineates the processes to be adhered to in case of non-performance, as well as the relative seniority of claims. As a consequence, the seniority of claims by creditors to sovereign nations is a matter of convention, which in turn determines the interest rates that are available to borrowers from different creditors. According to convention, multilateral creditors, including the IMF and World Bank, are treated as most senior, followed by bilateral creditors, and lastly by commercial creditors. It is worth noting that the preferred creditor status of the IMF is not based on any legal framework and is not mentioned in its Articles of Agreement. However, the IMF urges economies to confer preferred status on its lending, and its status is reinforced by bilateral lenders through the conventions of the Paris Club.

Empirical evidence is consistent with the convention that multilateral institutions enjoy the most senior status. However, there is evidence that, contrary to wisdom, official bilateral credit is junior (or at least not senior) to private sovereign debt such as bank loans and bonds. Private creditors typically get paid first and lose less than bilateral official creditors.[7] The evidence is, therefore, that defaults are selective, and some important factors influencing a sovereign's choice to default are based on the severity and visibility of the consequences. Defaults against the IMF and World Bank are the costliest because they cut off access to concessional lending during crises and may put a country's voting rights at risk. Conversely, the multilateral institutions have major incentives not to renegotiate their claims in order to protect their preferred creditor status. In comparison, defaults to bondholders are highly visible and can result in credit rating downgrades. However, defaults to bilateral lenders may be less transparent and based on renegotiations by governments that are influenced by other geopolitical factors.

Other factors influencing the likelihood of default include asymmetric information between creditors and debtors relating to the actual status of distress, and therefore the level of debt forgiveness that is appropriate. Under asymmetric information, a debtor is incentivized to misrepresent the severity of debt distress in order to win more generous relief. Therefore, creditors are also reluctant to offer debt relief, resulting in infrequent occurrences of debt forgiveness. The creditor may also consider the option of extending additional financing to the country under distress, with the hope that the cushion will support the country's recovery and enable it to pay back its obligations. Financing may be attractive to creditors because it provides them with an "option value", such that if the borrower ends up performing well, then the creditor will not have written down claims unnecessarily. However, the burden of debt distorts the debtor's incentives and increases the likelihood of underperformance since the benefits of good performance go largely to the creditor rather than to itself.

Indexation schemes that link repayment to a country's future output can result in better outcomes for both parties, as they remove the need for the debtor to truthfully reveal its private information. The index may comprise a variable that is either within the control of the country to a certain extent (such as exports or growth) or a variable that is outside its control (such as commodity prices). Research shows that private information and incentives make commodity price indexation preferable.[8] The development and use of contingent instruments has been constrained by a number of factors, including first-mover costs, difficulties in measuring and verifying contingencies and weak technical capacity, necessitating capacity building in order to deepen these markets.

Although developing economies within SSA and other parts of the world experienced varying degrees of debt distress and debt restructuring during the 1980s and 1990s, a major debate also arose within development circles on the responsibility for the debt crisis held by creditors themselves. The proponents of this debate posited that the outstanding debt was illegitimate on the basis of the failure by creditors to perform adequate due diligence prior to extending credit, and therefore that creditors should at least bear shared responsibility for failed lending. Or conversely, taking an analogy from private markets, individuals are not liable for debts incurred in their names by others through fraudulent means. Similarly, at the sovereign level, an analogous argument is made that sovereign debt incurred without the consent of the people and not benefitting a nation is illegitimate, and especially more so if creditors are aware of these facts in advance. Debt illegitimacy places emphasis on the creditor and is in stark contrast to the norm in international financial markets, where all renegotiations place emphasis on the obligations of the debtor. The notion of illegitimate or "odious" debt arose in 1898 after the Spanish-American War, when the United States repudiated Cuban liabilities to its colonial rulers on the basis that the debt had been incurred without the consent of the Cuban people and had not been used for their benefit.[9] However, in practice there is a low incidence of full repudiation of debt.[10]

The case for odious liabilities in Kenya can be debated in a number of instances throughout its history. During the colonial period, public liabilities were incurred for the benefit of European settlers, and public infrastructure was developed primarily in settlement areas. During the emergency period, additional debt was originated primarily to suppress the national struggle for independence. These liabilities, which were passed on to the nation upon independence, were not used for the benefit of Kenyan citizens. In more recent cases where massive corruption by leadership has diverted funds meant for development to private gain, there is also a clear loss incurred by citizens but an increased liability. Numerous other potential cases of odious debt are evidenced within SSA, of which one of the most prominent is the case of South Africa. Throughout the 1980s, South Africa's apartheid regime used financing obtained from private banks to oppress the African majority, and yet the same oppressed people are now responsible for the repayment of that debt. The power of the international financial architecture, where South Africa feared hurting its chances of accessing foreign finance, contributed to the government accepting responsibility for the debt.

A proposed solution to the issue of odious debt is the creation of an independent institution to assess the legitimacy of debt incurred by any given regime, and thereby restrict the ability of leaders to loot. It is posited that such an institution would enable countries to maintain their reputations and avoid sanctions in the event of refusing to pay illegitimate debts, in the same way that the reputation of an individual that refuses to pay fraudulent claims remains untarnished.[11] However, the authority of such an institution would be dependent either on its ability to enforce its decisions or on the willingness of countries to comply with its decisions. Additionally, the institution would require a framework to reinforce its independence from undue influence by sovereigns with incentives to seek repayment.

Despite the central role played by multilateral development institutions, particularly the IMF and World Bank, a major concern arises on the impartiality of their role in macroeconomic stability and economic development, given the structure of ownership, the norms underpinning leadership, and the voting rights of member economies. Voting rights within the institutions are highly in favor of American and European members, and the conventions of leadership for the two institutions are such that the head of the IMF is always European and the head of the World Bank is always American. These dynamics play a significant role in the perception across developing and emerging economies that the institutions are not impartial but rather instruments through which the policies of the West are promoted. An additional concern arises with the structure of IMF quotas, which provide a ceiling on a country's access to resources, beyond which it must pay higher charges and be subjected to greater oversight. This system was created under the prevalence of fixed exchange rate regimes, whereby larger economies would require greater levels of support to protect exchange rates relative to smaller economies. However, in a world where most economies have floating exchange rates, lending should be determined by the development needs and creditworthiness of economies.[12]

The new Kenyan Constitution was promulgated in August 2010 and resulted in the creation of a new subnational level of government with 47 counties, each with an elected governor, county executive and county assembly. The rationale for devolution was that decentralization would allow for improvement in service delivery through better preference matching, given the informational advantage that local governments would be expected to have over national government in terms of the demand for local public services, as well as providing citizens with the ability to exercise better control over their locally elected representatives, whom they would be better able to identify and hold accountable. However, evidence on the ability of decentralization to improve accountability is mixed. It may be difficult for a community to take action against elites, or elites may be able to influence enforcement processes, thereby diluting accountability.

Devolution has been accompanied with a transfer of functions to county governments, which are supported with a minimum unconditional transfer of 15 percent of shareable revenues to counties, with the distribution of revenues across counties determined by a revenue allocation formula. This transfer, known as the "equitable share", has significantly increased the flow of finance to regions that were previously underdeveloped, leading to significant development away from cities and creating some degree of insulation to regional funding from political influence at the national level. This has been a major win for equity by spurring regional growth and providing a base to allow regions to catch up to the major cities. However, there has been a costly duplication of efforts at the national and sub-national levels for some functions that were constitutionally devolved to the counties.

Further, the decentralization of functions has not been accompanied with decentralization of revenues. Ideally, taxes should be levied at a jurisdictional level consistent with the provision of public goods, and further, taxes should be designed to approximate a user fee at the local level.[13] This is important in matching the value that households attach to the provision of a given service to its cost in order to maximize the benefits achieved. However, regions within the country differ significantly in their ability to collect revenues locally, in large part also due to the historical uneven concentration of development efforts, making revenue decentralization difficult. The consequence has been partial decentralization that has created a significant vertical imbalance, whereby sub-national governments have considerably higher expenditures relative to revenues and where there is a high dependency on transfers from the central government. This imbalance generates a common pool problem, where sub-national governments, knowing that the central government will provide transfers, have incentives to spend more than is socially optimal. This problem is found to be more acute with a greater fiscal gap, which is the share of subnational revenues that are not financed through subnational tax collections.[14] Higher regional expenditures are reflected in larger overall fiscal deficits, which may prompt the central government to borrow more and therefore contribute to higher overall debt levels. Empirical evidence globally supports this intuition, whereby countries with greater vertical fiscal imbalances are also found to have higher overall public debt levels.[15]

Kenya's progress with decentralization has been achieved with a massive increase in sub-national expenditure, which has increased by 4 percentage points of GDP. Conversely, there has not been a matching decrease in spending at the national level. The major increase in spending has been in administrative costs, with the wage bill in particular accounting for the majority of recurrent expenditures in most counties. Overall, recurrent expenditures on average account for two-thirds of total expenditures within counties.[16]

Despite political economy reforms designed to increase the quality of governance, Kenya continues to face massive challenges in preventing the misappropriation of funds from citizens. Kenya is ranked low on the Corruption Perceptions Index and suffers immense social costs through foregone welfare-enhancing public investments. Institutional capacity to conclusively address corruption is severely limited by elite capture. To date, there are no successful prosecutions of individuals involved in high-profile corruption scandals. The occurrence of corruption is also aided by the availability of secrecy jurisdictions to which funds obtained through corrupt practices are channeled, whereby these jurisdictions facilitate the anonymity of global transfers. A major cost incurred by society is the great incentives that public officials face to approve and begin new public investment projects, whereby the approval process itself provides opportunities to earn significant rents through kickbacks from contractors bidding to win contracts. Officials are therefore incentivized to focus their efforts on the origination of large projects from which they can earn large payoffs, resulting in a massive misallocation of resources to projects that may not be social priorities, as well as compromising tender processes by awarding contracts to contractors that may not provide the highest value for money.

Funds obtained from corrupt practices are frequently channeled abroad and exert a major cost on the Kenyan economy. In general, illicit flows are difficult to detect, quantify and monitor due to their clandestine nature and due to a lack of information from the countries to which the funds are channeled. Further, the measurement of illicit flows has historically been fragmented and siloed. Today, there is no international framework that allows for continuous tracking and measurement of international illicit flows. However, the United Nations notes that with sufficient global cooperation, the statistical measurement and tracking of illicit flows is possible.[17] Global economic losses due to illicit activity are staggering. The United Nations finds that between 2 and 5 percent of global GDP is laundered each year, amounting to up to US$ 2 trillion annually.[18] These laundered proceeds are in turn obtained from other illicit or illegal activities, of which corruption alone makes a significant contribution. The occurrence of corrupt activities exerts a far greater magnitude of indirect costs through inefficient or value-destroying investments that do not meet the needs of society or through foregone investments that deny benefits but impose costs on society through repayment obligations.

The African Development Bank estimates that losses due to illicit financial flows in Africa amount to between US$ 50 billion and US$ 80 billion annually. In addition, up to 44 percent of Africa's financial wealth is held abroad.[19] The major practices that drive illicit activity are trade and tax abuse through tax avoidance and profit shifting, which account for 65 percent of the illicit flows. Criminal activity accounts for 25 percent of illicit flows, while the remaining 5 percent is due to corruption, including public officials and abuse of public office. External borrowing lost to corruption adds to the burden of payment for future generations. However, if these leakages were plugged, the need for external finance would be significantly reduced.

Notes

1 Gilens (2012).
2 Ohaegbulam (1992).
3 Swamy (1994).
4 IMF (1993), p. 3.
5 IMF (1997), p. 7.
6 IMF (1998), p. 9.
7 Schlegl et al. (2019).
8 See Froot et al. (1988) and Krugman (1988).
9 Jayachandran and Kremer (2006).
10 Luckner (2023), p. 12.
11 Jayachandran and Kremer (2006).
12 AfDB (2024), p. 177.
13 Musgrave (1959).
14 Gadenne and Singhal (2013).
15 Guo et al. (2022).
16 Statistics obtained from Kenya Office of Controller of Budget Reports.
17 United Nations (2022).
18 See United Nations Office on Drugs and Crime; www.unodc.org/unodc/en/money-laundering/overview.html.
19 See UN (2022), p. 5 and UNECA (2021), p. xv.

References

African Development Bank. *African Economic Outlook 2024: Driving Africa's Transformation. The Reform of the Global Financial Architecture*. 2024.

Froot, K., D. Scharfstein and J. Stein. *LDC Debt: Forgiveness, Indexation and Investment Incentives*. NBER Working Paper No. 2541, 1988.

Gadenne, L., and M. Singhal. "Decentralization in Developing Economies". *Annual Review of Economics* 6 (2013): 581–604.

Gilens, M. *Affluence and Influence: Economic Inequality and Political Power in America*. Princeton, NJ: Princeton University Press, 2012.

Guo, S., P. Yun and Z. Xie. *A Dynamic Model of Fiscal Decentralization and Public Debt Accumulation*. World Bank Working Paper No. 9927, 2022.

International Monetary Fund. *Kenya – Staff Report for the 1993 Article IV Consultation and Request for One-Year Arrangement Under the Enhanced Structural Adjustment Facility*. Report No. EBS/93/191. 1993.

International Monetary Fund. *Kenya – Staff Report for the 1996 Article IV Consultation*. SM/97/70. 1997.

International Monetary Fund. *Kenya – Staff Report for the 1998 Article IV Consultation*. SM/98/92. 1998.

Jayachandran, S., and M. Kremer. "Odious Debt." *American Economic Review* 96, no. 1 (2006): 82–92.

Krugman, P. *Financing vs. Forgiving a Debt Overhang*. NBER Working Paper No. 2486, 1988.

Luckner, C. G., J. Meyer, C. Reinhart and C. Trebesch. *Sovereign Debt: 200 Years of Creditor Losses*. Working Paper, 2023.

Musgrave, R. *The Theory of Public Finance*. New York: McGraw-Hill, 1959.

Ohaegbulam, U. "The United States and Africa after the Cold War." *Africa Today* 39, no. 4 (1992): 19–34.

Schlegl, M., C. Trebesch and M. Wright. *The Seniority Structure of Sovereign Debt*. NBER Working Paper No. 25793, 2019.

Swamy, G. *Kenya: Structural Adjustment in the 1980s*. World Bank Policy Research Working Paper No. 1238, 1994.

United Nations. Office of the Special Adviser on Africa. *Intensifying the Fight against Corruption and Money Laundering in Africa*. 2022.

United Nations Economic Commission for Africa. *Institutional Architecture to Address Illicit Financial Flows*. 2021.

9 Infrastructure Development, China and Private Debt Markets

Kenya has diversified its sources of public debt since the turn of the century through two major developments: borrowing from China and accessing sovereign bond markets. China has risen rapidly in prominence to become Kenya's major bilateral lending partner, with the majority of its loans used to finance major infrastructure projects. Kenya has also repeatedly accessed sovereign bond markets since obtaining a sovereign credit rating. Commercial debt as a consequence has increased to account for almost one-third of total external debt, with issuance in part encouraged by favorable international borrowing conditions following policy measures implemented by major monetary authorities globally to overcome the impact of the global financial crisis in 2008. However, the more diversified profile of Kenyan debt has raised new challenges in debt renegotiation across creditors. Bondholders are distributed and more difficult to negotiate with, and China is not a member of the Paris Club. In recent years, the importance of public-private partnerships (PPPs) as a model to finance public investment has been increasing in prominence.

Infrastructure is central to the development of any economy. Physical infrastructure, including roads, railway networks, ports and telecommunication networks, is critical to linking markets, enabling the provision of goods and services at a distance, and enabling the mobility of labor. Further, social infrastructure, including schools and hospitals, is essential for supporting human capital and improving productivity. Although Kenya's physical infrastructure is relatively developed in comparison to neighboring economies, it remains underdeveloped relative to upper middle- and high-income economies. There are also significant gaps in the comparative regional quality

DOI: 10.4324/9781003648826-10

of infrastructure, with lower levels of development in rural and arid areas of the country. For example, road network density is highest in central and western regions of the country, with the highest density in Nairobi. However, the road network density in arid areas is less than 2 percent that of Nairobi. Kenya's infrastructure development deficit is estimated at US$ 2 billion annually and is estimated to be responsible for up to 30 percent of the productivity handicap faced by Kenyan firms.[1] Evidence indicates that there are significant potential benefits to making quality investments in infrastructure. The rate of return to infrastructure investment is large, with estimates indicating that a 1 percent increase in infrastructure investment boosts private sector economic output by 0.17 percent in the long run.[2]

Infrastructure rarely satisfies the properties of a public good.[3] For example, road networks are neither non-rival nor non-excludable, meaning that individuals can be prevented from using a road through toll fees, and conversely, a congested road creates delays that diminish the experience of all road users. However, the following properties of infrastructure make public sector involvement central: first, infrastructure provides significant positive externalities, which are indirect benefits that all users enjoy as a result of the infrastructure; and second, it is typically too expensive and inefficient for competing producers to supply the same infrastructure, therefore making infrastructure a natural monopoly. Due to these properties, the government will typically take ownership of public infrastructure and be held accountable to citizens by providing value-for-money with infrastructure investments. The excludability and rivalry of public infrastructure allow the deployment of a number of financing models.

Public infrastructure investment can be financed through taxation, debt financing or PPPs. In a frictionless world, public finance theory posits that financing through revenue-raising or debt are equivalent. However, the significant up-front costs required for infrastructure investment increase the attractiveness of debt, given that development budgets at a national level may be substantially smaller than the financing necessary for infrastructure development and rehabilitation. However, debt instruments price in the risks inherent in infrastructure development and debt repayment. Ideally, the financing instrument matches the expected lifespan of the asset and the expected revenue streams, if any. Debt instruments are raised from three main sources: bilateral partners, multilateral partners and the private sector. Bilateral and multilateral partners are major sources of concessional financing for infrastructure, whereas the private sector provides loan financing or bonds through capital markets. The cost of borrowing across debt instruments is also influenced by insurance instruments such as guarantees, as well as structuring arrangements that spread the risks of the significant capital investment across multiple stakeholders.

Concessional borrowing has played a central historical role in financing the development of Kenya's infrastructure. However, concessional financing is limited relative to Kenya's infrastructure financing gap and raises the question of how it should most appropriately be channeled and utilized. Infrastructure investments across the country vary in profile by risk and public benefit. Within this spectrum, projects that have public benefit and low risk are the most attractive to both concessional and private sources of debt. Concessional financing targeted to commercially viable projects is cheaper and crowds out private financing, while leaving riskier projects with high public benefit unfinanced. A careful assessment of the additional cost of raising private capital for viable projects and the public benefits accruing from utilizing concessional financing for riskier and commercially unviable projects is key in maximizing the value of debt financing for infrastructure development.

Since the early 2000s, China's role in infrastructure financing has increased significantly across Africa. Chinese loans to Africa increased from close to US$ 1 billion in 2002 to over US$ 15 billion annually by 2013.[4] China's lending in Africa has been characterized by the promotion of resource-based lending and has placed a major emphasis on infrastructure investment in Africa, prompting large financing flows into the continent. Since 2010, Chinese investment has accounted for one-third of Africa's power grid and infrastructure financing, a trend that has also been mirrored in Kenya. Between 2001 and 2018, China lent approximately US$ 126 billion to African countries and invested US$ 41 billion in foreign direct investment.[5] In 2013, China's President Xi Jinping introduced China's Belt and Road Initiative (BRI), drawing inspiration from the Silk Road that flourished during the Han Dynasty. The BRI, which is a cornerstone of Chinese foreign policy, is an ambitious plan to develop trade routes connecting China with Africa and Europe through land and maritime networks to boost intercontinental trade and deepen regional integration.

Chinese lending to Africa is led by some key agencies. In the early 2000s, the major lending institution was China Exim Bank, a state-owned institution which is empowered to provide concessional loans to overseas projects and which has focused largely on infrastructure projects across the continent. China Exim Bank offers concessional loans with a considerable and competitive grant element to African economies, and lending is not tied to any political conditions, adhering to the Chinese principle of non-interference in the sovereign affairs of nation-states.[6] However, over time, the number of lending institutions, in particular those offering non-concessional loans, has increased. As of 2019, there were over 30 Chinese creditors offering loans in Africa, including the China Development Bank (CDB) and the Industrial and Commercial Bank of China (ICBC).[7]

Chinese investments have had a major impact on the relationship between African nations and sovereign lenders. In particular, China's status as a non-Paris Club economy has had significant ramifications. Paris Club members abide by a number of principles, including consensus across creditor countries on negotiation outcomes, conditionality on debt relief and regular information sharing on the status of debtor economies. As a non-member economy, China does not coordinate its debt restructuring with other economies, and neither does it share details of its contracts with its debtors. This has resulted in significant friction and mistrust between Paris Club lenders and China, with China accused of free-riding on the development efforts of the international community and impairing the debt sustainability of debtor economies.[8] Chinese investment in Africa has also resulted in greater alignment on geopolitical issues, as measured by greater convergence on voting at the United Nations, while at the same time a greater divergence has occurred on voting with the United States. Chinese policy has had a great impact on Western financing strategies, which over time have become more targeted at countering the influence of Chinese policies rather than addressing the major economic needs of African economies.[9]

Trends in Kenya have mirrored those on the rest of the continent as Chinese influence has transformed the infrastructure finance landscape (Figure 9.1). Ramping up from modest lending at the turn of the century, Kenya's outstanding debt to China increased from KES 4 billion in 2008 to KES 32 billion in 2011, as China's role in Kenya's infrastructure increased with the commissioning of projects, including the Nairobi-Thika Superhighway. In particular, Chinese investments in Kenya have been mainly concentrated in the transport and energy sectors over this period, leading to improvements in infrastructure quality. China's first investment in Kenya under the BRI was the

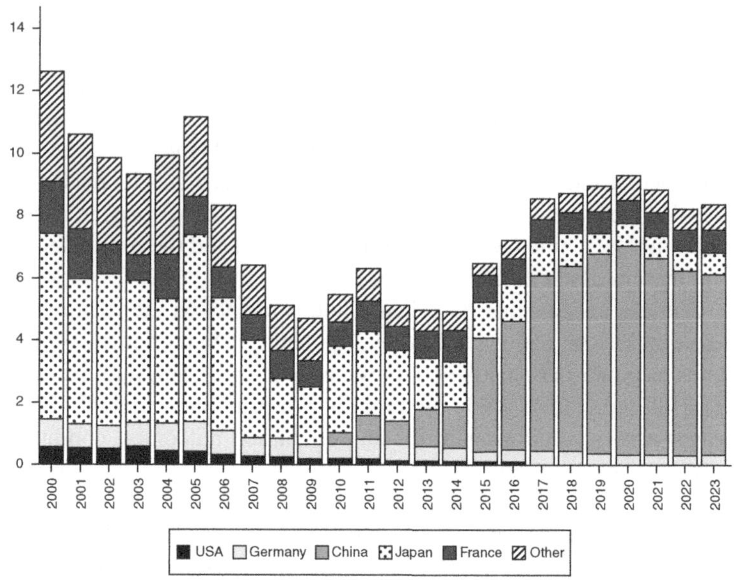

Figure 9.1 External bilateral debt by country (percent of GDP).
Source: Data from Kenya National Bureau of Statistics, Economic Surveys, 2005–2024.

Standard Gauge Railway (SGR), which was envisioned as part of a larger regional project within the East African Community (EAC) to improve transportation links in Kenya, Uganda, South Sudan, Ethiopia and D.R. Congo. The EAC adopted the international standard gauge as the norm for the railway, which was selected to handle the projected growth in regional trade.[10] The SGR cost US$ 3.6 billion as of 2018, borrowed from China Exim Bank.[11] The project became embroiled in a debt-trap diplomacy narrative in 2018, when the East African newspaper published an article which claimed that Mombasa Port had been put up as collateral for the Chinese loan, thereby putting the strategic asset at risk of seizure by the Chinese government in case of default. These allegations led to the partial publication of details of the SGR contract, a departure from the norm whereby contract details on bilateral debt agreements are kept private.

Chinese investments have contributed to creating a skewed trade relationship between Kenya and China. Between 2015 and 2019, total trade between Kenya and China amounted to US$ 18.2 billion, where the share of Kenyan imports from China was 97 percent of the total, while Kenyan exports to China accounted for the remaining meager 3 percent. Further, between 2005 and 2019, Kenya facilitated over 300 Chinese investment projects with a total value exceeding US$ 1.5 billion.[12] These major investments are one of the major contributing factors to the surge in Kenya's public debt level. After a period of declining overall debt in the 2000s, debt levels trended back upwards to above 50 percent of GDP in 2019 prior to the COVID-19 pandemic, with the composition of external debt increasing.

In addition to the impact of Chinese investment, the increase in infrastructure investment in Kenya and other African economies was supported by a prevailing ideology supported by multilateral organizations and the international community, which pushed for larger investments in infrastructure. In 2014, the G20 noted the critical need to tackle global investment and infrastructure shortfalls in order to lift growth and productivity, as well as to create jobs.[13]

However, investments in infrastructure projects have also demonstrated some acute inefficiencies, as evidenced by delays in project commencement after the signing of financing agreements, stalled and incomplete projects, in part evidenced by low disbursement rates, or projects completed to a poor standard or not meeting the needs of their intended beneficiaries. This poor performance calls into question the value for money achieved by citizens from public investments. Inefficiencies have led to a sprawling portfolio of publicly funded projects. Between 2020 and 2023, the Government of Kenya paid KES 5.4 billion in commitment fees for undisbursed loans, which were incurred due to the approval for financing of projects without proper planning or preparedness. The major factors that contribute to poor performance on investments include inadequate counterpart financing as required by loan agreements, in addition to operational inefficiencies in ensuring that compensation and disputes for projects that require land acquisition and resettlement are completed prior to signing financing agreements.[14] This requires an efficient framework for collaboration across all stakeholders involved in externally funded projects to ensure efficient coordination during project planning, approval and implementation in order to avoid delays.

Additionally, other key factors contributing to poor project performance include limited public participation with the intended beneficiaries of projects in order to ensure ownership and clear alignment with their needs, inadequate evaluation and negotiation for favorable credit terms, and limited monitoring and evaluation of projects. For stalled or non-performing projects, the National Treasury does not have an adequate framework in place for the prompt cancellation of such projects, and neither do the National Treasury and relevant implementing agencies ensure negotiation for the provision of exit clauses on favorable terms within financing agreements, in addition to ensuring that prepayment penalties are minimized. These gaps contribute to the continued payment of penalties on non-performing projects and also contribute to an inability to free up resources that could in turn enable the redeployment of financing to other viable projects.[15]

The global financial crisis in 2007 had a significant impact on opening international commercial markets for debt to Africa. In the mid-2000s, markets for securitized mortgages boomed in Western economies, with investment banks pooling household mortgage portfolios into structured finance instruments that re-packaged repayment risk into tiers and which were then re-sold to investors based on risk profile. This process of securitization led to the rise of the subprime mortgage market, where mortgages were originated to low-income buyers and securitized across a spectrum of investors, with institutional investors purchasing the most secure tranches based on expected cash flows, and hedge funds purchasing the riskiest tranches, which also provided the highest returns. Moral hazard problems, whereby organizations originating subprime mortgages did not have proper incentives to price in the risk of origination—given that they on-sold their portfolios—contributed to excessive risk-taking that eventually culminated in the largest global financial crisis since the Great Depression in the 1920s. The crisis was ignited with the collapse of Lehman Brothers, a major investment bank, in 2008. Global financial markets seized up as a result and prompted a major coordinated response by central banks in advanced economies.

In order to shore up global liquidity and to prevent advanced economies from slipping into deflation, the United States Treasury and the European Central Bank launched quantitative easing programs through which they purchased significant portfolios of non-performing assets and at the same time channeled unprecedented levels of liquidity into the financial sector. These stimulus measures dropped real interest rates in advanced economies to below zero and lowered yields on investments by institutional investors. The consequent low interest rates on international debt provided an opportunity for African economies to tap international commercial markets for finance. The search for yield by institutional investors contributed to the diversification of their portfolios globally. African economies were able to attract global investors with sovereign bond issuances, thereby changing the landscape of borrowing across the continent. Bond issuances in Africa increased from US$ 10 billion annually in the early 2000s to about US$ 80 billion annually by 2016, leading the share of commercial debt in Africa to increase from 17 percent of total debt in 2000 to 43 percent by 2021.[16]

Entry into sovereign bond markets is contingent on the availability of an independent third-party assessment of creditworthiness. Credit rating agencies play a central role in providing this information. Credit ratings perform the important function of aggregating information about the credit quality of sovereigns and providing a public assessment of credit risk. This assessment overcomes information constraints and lowers the costs of monitoring the quality of debt for investors, thereby increasing the transferability of debt across third parties and supporting the liquidity of bond markets. By signaling the creditworthiness of a given country to international capital markets, sovereign ratings play a critical role in influencing borrowing costs, whereby higher credit ratings translate into lower costs and vice versa. Ratings changes can have a significant effect on the costs of access to capital. In particular, the transition between investment and speculative grade ratings has an impact on credit spreads and therefore access to debt markets.[17] The rise of credit ratings coincided with the expansion of sovereign bond markets in the 1990s, as these markets largely replaced syndicated loans globally, which are loans extended by a group of financial institutions.

In contrast, sovereign loans typically involve a costly private assessment of debt by the lender or lending syndicate, which is kept private. As a consequence, markets for sovereign loans are less liquid. An important distinction across both markets is therefore that banks tend to act as "private" monitors of credit risk while credit rating agencies act as "public" monitors of credit risk. As markets for commercial debt have evolved, the roles played by sovereign bonds and syndicated loans have also changed. Evidence shows that the average maturity of sovereign bonds is higher than that of syndicated loans. The transferability of bonds makes them cheaper for long-term finance relative to loans, as their liquidity supports the uncertainty of future payments. Conversely, the limited number of creditors that issue syndicated loans support easier negotiations to roll over the debt. Thus, syndicated loans are optimally used for short-term debt and bonds for longer term debt.[18]

The access to markets for commercial bonds in Africa is in line with a global shift to a larger share of sovereign debt in commercial lending relative to sovereign loans. This shift carries the benefit of increasing the number of participants in sovereign lending, thereby lowering the concentration of risk to a smaller number of banks and increasing the liquidity of the bonds. Commercial debt markets have also proved attractive due to the lack of conditionality. Additionally, sovereign bonds are more transparent, and their pricing reflects an assessment of risk at any given moment in time. However, these properties also make sovereign bonds more difficult to renegotiate, as their ownership is more distributed and complex. Further, the issuance of bonds increases the importance of sovereign credit ratings, on which investors place emphasis in deciding portfolio allocations.

Kenya attained a sovereign rating in order to support access to sovereign bond markets. The first rating was issued by Standard and Poor's in 2006 and introduced at below investment grade.[19] Fitch Ratings followed with its rating in 2007.[20] Kenya's issuance of sovereign bonds increased rapidly after the global financial crisis in 2008, which in turn increased the total share of commercial debt. Prior to 2008, the share of commercial debt in Kenya's total external debt averaged less than 5 percent. However, by 2019, the share of commercial debt rose to approximately one-third of total external debt (Figure 9.2). The key issuances were sovereign bonds on European markets. The first sovereign Eurobond raised by Kenya was issued in June 2014 for US$ 2 billion, the largest for an African sovereign at the time excluding South Africa. Following this issuance, a second Eurobond was issued in December 2014 for US$ 750 million, and additional issuances raised US$ 2 billion in February 2018 and US$ 2.1 billion in May 2019, prior to the COVID-19 pandemic.[21] Kenya also sold its first infrastructure bond in 2009 and followed the successful issuance with further bonds. Additionally, Kenya increasingly tapped commercial markets through the issuance of syndicated loans. In October 2015, Kenya contracted a US$ 750 million syndicated loan and further contracted two syndicated loans in 2019 for US$ 250 million and US$ 1.25 billion, respectively.[22]

Besides the evolution of debt markets, a major financing tool that has also gained prominence in infrastructure financing within Kenya

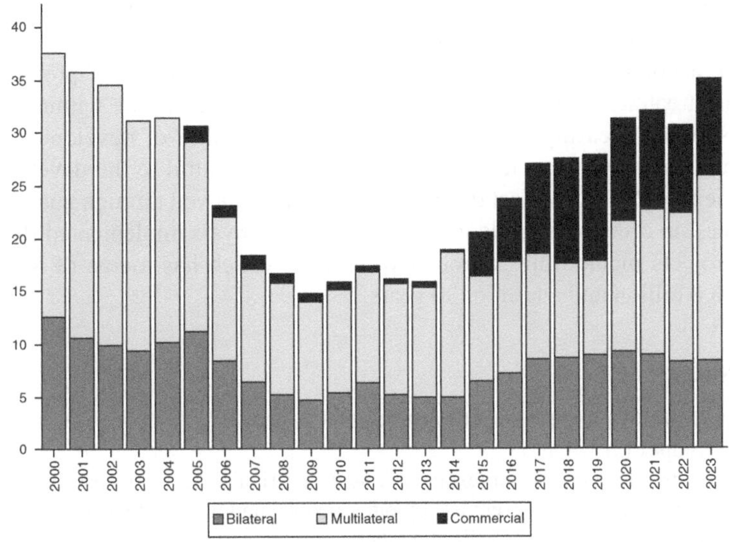

Figure 9.2 External debt by source (percent of GDP).

Source: Data from Kenya National Bureau of Statistics, Economic Surveys, 2005–2024. Commercial debt includes international sovereign bonds, commercial banks and suppliers' credit.

is PPPs. These partnerships are contractual agreements between a government contracting authority and a private organization, whereby the organization undertakes to perform a public function or provide a service on behalf of the government for a specified period of time, during which the organization is generally liable for risks arising from its performance of the function in return for a benefit received from a public fund or from fees charged to consumers. A number of incentives motivate governments to enter PPP agreements, including the need to attract private capital to fill significant financing gaps in infrastructure investment that cannot be filled with limited public sources of finance; the intention to increase the operational efficiency with which projects are run by bringing on board an entity with capacity and experience in managing a given type of project; and the desire to improve the allocational efficiency with which resources are deployed, including crowding in the private sector for financially viable projects and allocating a greater share of public resources toward public goods.

From a public debt perspective, a significant impact of the development of PPP projects is the off-balance sheet treatment of projects, which allows the government to maintain fiscal sustainability from an accounting perspective, whereby risks arising from PPP projects are treated as contingent claims. Kenya's PPP directorate within the National Treasury is tasked with the responsibility of developing a pipeline of projects that are viable for PPPs. Central to the development of PPPs is project de-risking, typically achieved through guarantees, in order to provide investor comfort. Kenya's implemented PPP projects include the Nairobi Expressway, which has a cost of KES 86.8 billion and a term of 30 years.[23]

Notes

1 World Bank (2018) and Briceño-Garmedia (2010), p. 3.
2 Stupak (2018), p. 13.
3 A public good is non-excludable and non-rivalrous, where use by one person does not prevent use by other people, and neither does use by one person decrease availability to others.
4 Boston University, Chinese Loans to Africa Database, 2024.
5 Foreign Policy Research Institute, *Chinese Economic Engagement in Africa: Implications for U.S. Policy* (January 2022).
6 On average, Chinese loans have an interest rate of 3.6 percent, a grace period of 4 years, and a maturity of 12 years, representing a grant element of around 36 percent. See Executive Research Associates (2009).
7 Usman (2021).
8 OECD (2007).
9 Foreign Policy Research Institute, *Chinese Economic Engagement in Africa: Implications for U.S. Policy* (January 2022).
10 China-Africa Research Initiative (2022).
11 China-Africa Research Initiative (2022), p. 4.
12 Mercator Institute for China Studies (2022).
13 G20 Leaders' Communique, Brisbane Summit (November 2014).
14 Office of the Auditor-General (2023).
15 Office of the Auditor-General (2022).
16 ADB Speech by Dr. Adesina to Paris Club, *Evolution of the Debt Landscape over the Past 10 Years in Africa* (June 20, 2023).
17 IMF (2010), Chapter 3.
18 See Tanaka (2005).
19 See Standard and Poor's Global, "Sovereign Ratings History"; www.spglobal.com/ratings/en/research/articles/210726-sovereign-ratings-history-12029439. Kenya's transfer and convertibility assessment as of September 8, 2006 was BB.

20 Fitch Ratings introduced Kenya's sovereign rating on December 12, 2007, with a long-term issuer default rating of B+ (stable). See Fitch Ratings, "Kenya: Ratings"; www.fitchratings.com/entity/kenya-86485911#ratings.
21 IMF (May 2020).
22 IMF (April 2020), pp. 3–4.
23 See Kenya Public Private Partnership Directorate, "Delivering Sustainable Investments: Nairobi Expressway"; https://pppkenya.go.ke/ova_por/nairobi-expressway/.

References

Briceño-Garmendia, C. M., and M. Shkaratan. *Kenya's Infrastructure: A Continental Perspective*. World Bank, 2010.
China-Africa Research Initiative. *How Africa Borrows from China: Why Mombasa Port Is Not Collateral for Kenya's SGR*. 2022.
Executive Research Associates. *China in Africa: A Strategic Overview*. 2009.
International Monetary Fund. *Global Financial Stability Report: Sovereigns, Funding and Systemic Liquidity*. 2010.
International Monetary Fund. *Kenya – Request for Disbursement under the Rapid Credit Facility*. IMF Country Report No. 20/156, May 2020.
International Monetary Fund. *Kenya – Requests for an Extended Arrangement under the Extended Fund Facility and an Arrangement under the Extended Credit Facility*. IMF Country Report No. 21/72, April 2021.
Mercator Institute for China Studies. *Beyond Blocs: Global Views on China and US-China Relations*. August 2022.
Office of the Auditor General. *Performance Audit Report of the Auditor-General on Public Debt Servicing Activities*. 2022.
Office of the Auditor General. *Auditor General's Performance Audit Report on Contracting of External Loans for Public Development Projects*. 2023.
Organization for Economic Cooperation and Development. *Is China Actually Helping to Improve Debt Sustainability in Africa*. G-24 Policy Brief No. 9, 2007.
Stupak, J. M. *Economic Impact of Infrastructure Investment*. Congressional Research Service, 2018.
Tanaka, M. *Bank Loans versus Bond Finance: Implications for Sovereign Debtors*. Bank of England Working Paper No. 267, 2005.
Usman, Zainab. *What Do We Know about Chinese Lending in Africa?* Carnegie Endowment for International Peace, 2021.
World Bank. *Kenya: Enabling Private-Sector Participation in Infrastructure and Social Services*. March 2018.

10 Debt Considerations for the 21st Century

Kenya's history of debt shows a transition in terms of the development of debt markets and debt instruments, with the mobilization and deepening of both external and domestic sources of finance. Additionally, social and economic policies have contributed to better social outcomes, including better educational and health outcomes, while the population growth rate has declined from more than 4 percent to about 2 percent. Further, a framework for sound macroeconomic management has been established through the implementation of an inflation-targeting regime. However, a number of fundamental issues still remain. The Kenyan economy is characterized by low private savings, low productivity and declining competitiveness in international trade. Governance issues are pervasive, with corruption a major enduring concern.[1] The share of Kenya's informal sector has increased to almost 85 percent, with informal businesses lacking adequate support in terms of financial services. Further, the contribution of Kenya's exports to growth has declined from almost 20 percent following independence to less than 10 percent over the last decade. Additionally, Kenya's terms of trade have been constantly declining, an outcome of the long-standing inability to provide value addition in exports while at the same time maintaining dependency on value-added imports whose relative prices consistently increase in comparison to raw exports.

Developing economies have seen a rapid increase in debt since the mid-2010s. Overall debt levels have risen in SSA, driven by a variety of factors, including cheap international finance and China's foreign policy objectives. On average, public debt levels rose from 29 percent of GDP in 2012 to 59 percent of GDP by 2022.[2] The

DOI: 10.4324/9781003648826-11

global economy has suffered some major shocks since 2020, beginning with the COVID-19 pandemic, which resulted in a severe loss of life with its onset and prompted the implementation of social distancing, quarantine and curfew measures to limit the spread of the virus as the health sector raced to develop an effective vaccine. The measures disrupted international trade and pushed the global economy into recession. Advanced economies took extraordinary measures to support households and stimulate demand, but developing economies, already with high levels of debt, had limited fiscal space to implement demand stimulus. The global recession reversed gains that had been made in lowering poverty rates across the world and pushed more than 100 million people into extreme poverty.[3]

In response to the pandemic, the IMF and World Bank set up the Debt Service Suspension Initiative (DSSI) in May 2020, with the objective of enabling countries to utilize resources that would otherwise be used to pay debt to fight the pandemic and safeguard the lives of vulnerable individuals. The DSSI was active between May 2020 and December 2021 and suspended US$ 12.9 billion in debt service payments owed by 48 countries that chose to participate out of the eligible 73 countries. Kenya initially did not participate in the DSSI due to fears that a clause in its outstanding Eurobonds could see debt relief interpreted as a default event and potentially trigger a full loan recall. A contractual clause empowered 25 percent of bondholders to trigger a recall of the entire loan and interest in the event of a default, which included failure to pay any external debt or actions including declaring a moratorium on the payment of principal or interest on external debt.[4] Kenya eventually participated in the DSSI in 2021 but only participated until June of the year. During this period, the total debt relief obtained amounted to US$ 504 million, equivalent to 0.46 percent of GDP.[5]

Recognizing the need for strong coordination amongst creditors in addressing debt vulnerabilities in countries with high levels of public debt, the G20 set out a common framework for the treatment of debt beyond the DSSI in order to facilitate orderly and timely payment of debt by DSSI-eligible countries, with the intention of including broad participation by all creditors, including the private sector. The goal of the common framework was to deal with insolvency and protracted liquidity problems in conjunction with implementing an IMF-supported reform program. The common framework also required participation by private creditors on comparable terms with official creditors in order to overcome collective action challenges and ensure equal burden sharing. However, participation in the framework has been limited, with only a handful of countries opting to participate. The inclusion of new creditors that now comprise a significant share of debt to developing countries has complicated the implementation of the framework and limited confidence in its ability to serve as an effective platform for debt reform.

Following the COVID-19 pandemic, the global economy experienced additional shocks that further weighed on the debt obligations of developing economies, pushing 9 economies into debt distress and placing 25 economies at high risk of debt distress as of 2024. At the end of 2023, Kenya was listed as an economy at high risk of debt distress, with its debt-to-GDP ratio climbing to 73 percent and debt service consuming 55 percent of government revenues.[6] In February 2022, Russia invaded Ukraine in an incursion that resulted in a rapid increase in commodity prices for fuel, fertilizer, wheat and other foodstuffs. These price increases resulted in higher levels of food and fuel inflation that weighed particularly on households. Additionally, the United States and the European Union began to see higher levels of inflation that prompted their monetary authorities to raise interest rates aggressively, prompting a significant rebalancing of portfolios and resulting in capital outflows to advanced economies that led to a significant depreciation of the Kenyan shilling. As a consequence, debt repayment obligations in foreign currency increased even further and exerted additional strain on the already high levels of debt repayment obligations. The high interest rates contributed to an increase in lending rates on international bond markets, making refinancing of outstanding sovereign debt significantly more expensive. This increased the risk faced by sovereigns in refinancing bonds upon maturity when large principal payments are due. For example, Kenya's Eurobond was refinanced in February 2024 at an interest rate of 9.75 percent, significantly higher than the coupon of 6.875 percent that the newly originated debt was partially used to buy back.[7]

Despite the major constraints with debt repayments, interest rates on external bilateral and multilateral finance in particular are lower than those on domestic borrowing. Additionally, concessional finance obtained from multilateral institutions continues to be the cheapest form of financing available for investment in public goods. Therefore, borrowing from multilateral institutions continues to be a major component of Kenya's outstanding debt, contributing to a large share of external liabilities denominated in foreign currency.

Kenya has, since 2019, tapped the World Bank's Development Policy Financing (DPF) instrument, which has become a major channel through which the country has obtained concessional multilateral financing. The DPF is structured to provide rapidly disbursing financing in order to assist the borrower with addressing actual or anticipated development financing needs.[8] Unlike project financing, which provides funds for the implementation of specific projects, the DPF provides fungible financing or "non-earmarked, general budget financing that is subject to the borrower's own implementation processes and systems".[9] However, access to funds is contingent on the implementation of policy and institutional actions. Critically, the instrument requires the fulfillment of prior actions before the disbursement of funds, which are policy and institutional reforms or actions deemed critical to supporting the achievement of program objectives. The DPF emphasizes country ownership over the specific policies supported by the operation but makes an independent assessment of whether the policies are likely to have a significant impact on poverty and the environment.

Kenya's first DPF was approved in 2019 for an amount of US$ 750 million, the first in a programmatic series of two operations. Since then, a number of additional operations have been approved, including US$ 1 billion in March 2020, US$ 750 million in March 2022, US$ 1 billion in May 2023 and US$ 1.2 billion in May 2024. The DPOs have been implemented with commitments toward policy and institutional reforms across various areas, including creating fiscal space to support transparent spending and fiscal consolidation; implementing reforms in the electricity sector and reforming the framework for public-private partnerships; boosting competitiveness in agricultural exports and fostering more competitive and inclusive labor markets; strengthening climate action; and strengthening transparency and accountability.[10] While DPOs provide flexibility by allowing an economy to spend fungible funds in return for executing prior policy reforms, the monitoring of expenditure is more difficult. Additionally, it is not clear if reforms passed prior to accessing funds are at risk of reversal once funds are accessed or if barriers may prevent the operational implementation of reforms even if legal frameworks and regulations are implemented.

Like many African economies, Kenya is highly vulnerable to the impacts of climate change. Throughout its history, the economy has experienced severe impacts on growth as a consequence of climate shocks, and policy actions to bolster its resilience to adverse climate events have had a limited impact. Like other economies, particularly in SSA, climate vulnerability indices, which quantify the exposure of a given country to climate events and its capacity to adapt, reveal a low level of preparedness in comparison to other parts of the world. These vulnerabilities are in part a consequence of underlying structural issues, including the quality of infrastructure providing food, water and health care.

Due to increasingly volatile global climate patterns, climate policies have become central. It is important to distinguish climate adaptation policies from mitigation policies. Climate adaptation refers to actions that are taken to reduce vulnerability to climate change, including a broad range of structural, institutional, ecological or behavioral actions. In contrast, climate mitigation policies aim to reduce the causes of climate change, such as greenhouse gas emissions. SSA economies are low greenhouse gas emitters, and the bulk of the continent's financing needs are in climate adaptation. In contrast, advanced economies account for the largest share of greenhouse gas emissions and have major needs in climate mitigation. Global financing patterns mirror the needs of advanced economies and are directed toward climate mitigation. Between 2021 and 2022, total global climate finance amounted to about US$ 1.27 trillion, of which climate adaptation received only US$ 63 billion (less than 5 percent of total financing), in comparison to mitigation activities that received US$ 1,150 billion.[11] There has been a large increase in adaptation financing, which has reached an all-time high in nominal terms. However, as a share of total climate finance, it still falls far short of the adaptation needs of developing economies alone, which are estimated to amount to between US$ 212–387 billion a year by 2030.[12] In Africa, the mobilization of climate adaptation finance amounts to only about one-fifth of total financing needs.

Global adaptation finance is dominated by public sector funding, which accounts for 98 percent of total flows. Project debt raised at market rates accounts for 59 percent of total climate finance originated, while low-cost project debt and grants account for 21 percent and 17 percent of flows, respectively. Additionally, almost 50 percent of total adaptation finance is directed to water and sanitation projects (CPI, 2023). Within Africa, there is also a large dependence on international finance, which accounts for 92 percent of total flows and which is obtained in large part from multilateral development institutions, in comparison to other regions of the world that have a more balanced split between domestic and international flows.[13]

Debt repayment obligations are constraining the ability of African economies, including Kenya, to invest sufficiently in climate adaptation. There is therefore a major need and a major opportunity to develop and implement solutions that address the dual challenges of debt fragility and the climate adaptation investment gap. A significant opportunity also exists to leverage global climate commitments in order to achieve climate adaptation objectives. However, it is also critical to increase the participation of the private sector, which makes a marginal contribution to climate finance, amounting to less than 3 percent of adaptation flows. Even of this small percentage, a substantial proportion is accounted for by philanthropic funds. The constraints limiting private investment in climate adaptation include the lack of a pipeline of financially viable and bankable climate adaptation projects, incomplete knowledge on the costs of climate risks and gaps in the measurability of returns to investors.[14]

In addition to crowding in private investment, there is an increase in the utilization of debt-for-nature swaps in order to overcome debt overhang while committing investments to adaptation. These swaps build on the debt-for-development swaps that grew in the 1980s. Debt-for-nature swaps include bipartite and tripartite transactions, where the former are limited to agreements between a debtor government and one or more creditor governments, and the latter include the participation of non-governmental organizations in addition to the debtor and creditor governments. Over the last decade, Seychelles completed a debt-for-nature swap in 2016 in a tripartite transaction including the Nature Conservancy.[15] This transaction was followed in 2023 by Gabon, which refinanced US$ 500 million of the country's national debt while generating US$ 163 million in new funding for ocean conservation. The approach to retiring old debt is increasingly toward auctions, with Barbados, Ecuador and Gabon using modified Dutch auctions to buy back part of existing bonds.[16] These auctions lower the costs associated with implementing swaps by providing a market-based alternative to costly negotiations. With modified Dutch auctions, submitted bid tenders specify a combination of bond volumes and bid prices, effectively delineating a demand curve for each tender within a specific range provided by the auctioning government.

However, the market for debt-for-climate swaps remains limited, even in the case where existing debt obligations of a given economy are trading at a discount, due to the relative seniority between climate investments and the servicing of outstanding debt. In this case, even though debt may be deeply discounted, some of the benefits of debt-for-climate swaps accrue to non-participating creditors, thereby making them less efficient to support than conditional grants. If existing debt and climate investment are ranked the same in seniority, or if climate investment ranks junior to existing debt, then the expected value of debt relief through the implementation of a swap will be lower than its face value in the case where a country defaults on its outstanding debt, as some of the debt relief will be diverted to pay off existing creditors. Thus, the full value of a climate investment is unlikely to be realized in the case of default, and the climate investment will be unlikely to occur.[17]

The continued vulnerability of the Kenyan economy to macroeconomic shocks makes a case for the issuance of state-contingent debt instruments (SCDIs). These instruments have been in existence for some time as a countercyclical and risk-sharing tool but have had limited uptake, particularly in developing economies. The major benefit of SCDIs is their explicit link of debt servicing to indicators of a sovereign's ability to pay, and therefore providing for an automatic increase in fiscal space during bad times. By doing so, these instruments provide a cushion against debt distress and may also increase debt-carrying capacity. The development of SCDI markets, particularly within developing economies, faces some constraints that need policy interventions to overcome. These include a first-mover problem, where, prior to the deepening of markets, a high novelty and liquidity premium may be demanded by investors in the early stage of market development. There is therefore a role for international financial institutions to play in developing the market for these instruments in order to incentivize widespread adoption.

Additionally, the impact of shocks on exchange rates makes a case for higher levels of local currency financing in order to hedge against foreign exchange risk. Issuance of local currency debt requires the development of domestic debt markets to crowd in sources of finance, including pension funds and diaspora remittances, while at the same time avoiding the risk of crowding out lending to the private sector.

The G-20 has advocated a larger role for multilateral development banks such as the African Development Bank in boosting finance by shifting their portfolios from an originate-and-hold to an originate-and-distribute model, thus focusing on their comparative advantage in project preparation, technical assistance and overseeing project implementation.[18] Foreign currency risk can be mitigated through the placement of development bank portfolios in local currency with institutional investors with appropriate profiles.[19] In addition to local currency financing, the development of export markets is critical not just as an engine of economic growth but as a source of foreign exchange, serving as an effective buffer against negative currency movements.

The history of public debt illustrates a dual experience for the Kenyan economy. On the one hand, debt has played a role in supporting development and has been critical in particular during ambitious development phases implemented in the 1970s and the mid-2000s. These periods contributed to an improvement in living standards and a decline in overall poverty while increasing the quality of infrastructure. However, public debt has itself been responsible for periods of economic and social distress when debt sustainability has declined due to large repayment obligations. In Kenya's history, the major periods of debt fragility have occurred in the 1980s and the 2020s and have been preceded by large accumulations of debt for development. However, the high level of debt did not itself precipitate debt fragility. A major role has been played by the occurrence of shocks, which magnify the exposure of the economy. The shocks themselves are recurrent in nature, frequently stemming from climate events or global commodity prices, especially oil prices. Despite their likelihood of recurrence, Kenya has been unable to build sufficient resilience against their impact.

Over the medium term, despite the progress Kenya has made in economic development, there is an evident failure of the economy to maximize value addition from debt. A decline in governance and accountability has led to delays in the implementation of public investment projects, poor completion rates and substandard quality in many cases where projects have been implemented. Citizens view corruption as a major barrier to development. Additionally, productivity levels in the economy remain low, and the informal sector has grown to account for most jobs in the economy.

Improvements in value-for-money and debt sustainability demand deliberate efforts to address challenges illustrated by Kenya's history of public debt. Debt will continue to be a central and necessary tool for Kenya's development. However, Kenya's policies must demand accountability for public debt by enforcing penalties for the misappropriation of borrowed funds. Additionally, the country must build resilience to both domestic and external shocks, which have repeatedly contributed to debt fragility. Domestically, this requires building resilience in particular to climate events and improving the depth of domestic debt markets in order to lower the exposure to exchange-rate movements. However, global financial infrastructure also has a role to play by increasing the availability of instruments that account for macroeconomic shocks, such as SCDIs. Further, international creditors have a role to play in ensuring adequate due diligence on originated debt so that borrowed funds are deployed for the benefit of all citizens.

Notes

1 Afrobarometer (2022).
2 IMF (2023).
3 See World Bank, "Debt Service Suspension Initiative", March 10, 2022; www.worldbank.org/en/topic/debt/brief/covid-19-debt-service-suspension-initiative.
4 See Clause 10 of the Sovereign Bond Prospectus dated 26 February 2028.
5 IMF (2022), p. 9.
6 IMF (2024), p. 9.
7 See Business Daily, *Kenya Pays Dearly to Avoid Sh 316bn Eurobond Default* (February 14, 2024).
8 World Bank, *Development Policy Financing*; www.worldbank.org/en/what-we-do/products-and-services/financing-instruments/development-policy-financing.
9 World Bank, *Development Policy Financing.*
10 See World Bank, "Kenya Receives a $750 Million Boost to Support Economic Transformation Post-Pandemic", March 16, 2022: www.worldbank.org/en/news/press-release/2022/03/16/kenya-receives-a-750-million-boost-to-support-economic-transformation-post-pandemic; World Bank, "Kenya Taps $1 Billion Support for Fiscal Consolidation Efforts and Other Key Policy Reforms", May 30, 2023: www.worldbank.org/en/news/press-release/2023/05/26/kenya-afe-taps-1-billion-support-for-fiscal-consolidation-efforts-and-other-key-policy-reforms; World Bank, "Kenya: New Financing to Address Fiscal Pressures and Accelerate Inclusive and Green Growth", May 30, 2024: www.worldbank.org/en/news/press-release/2024/05/30/kenya-afe-new-financing-to-address-fiscal-pressures-and-accelerate-inclusive-and-green-growth.
11 CPI (2023).

12 There are large variances in the estimation of climate adaptation needs. Climate Policy Initiative estimates are US$ 212 billion per year in comparison to UNEP estimates of US$ 215–387 billion a year until 2030 (UNEP, 2023).
13 CPI (2023).
14 Adhikari and Chalkasra (2021).
15 Fontana-Raina and Grund (2023).
16 Jain et al. (2023).
17 Chamon et al. (2022).
18 G-20 (2022).
19 FSD Africa (2024).

References

Adhikari, B., and L. Chalkasra. "Mobilizing Private Sector Investment for Climate Action: Enhancing Ambition and Scaling Up Implementation." *Journal of Sustainable Finance and Investment* 13, no. 2 (2023): 1110–27.

Afrobarometer. *Afrobarometer Round 9 Summary of Results for Kenya.* 2022.

Chamon, C., E. Klok, V. Thakoor and J. Zettelmeyer. *Debt-for-Climate Swaps: Analysis, Design and Implementation.* International Monetary Fund, Working Paper WP/22/162, 2022.

Climate Policy Initiative, and Global Center on Adaptation. *State and Trends in Climate Adaptation Finance, 2023.* CPI, 2023.

Fontana-Raina, S., and S. Grund. *Debt-for-Nature Swaps: The Belize 2021 Deal and the Future of Green Sovereign Finance*. 2023.

FSD Africa. *Local Currency Solution for Multilateral Development Bank Portfolio Transfer: Feasibility Study*. 2024.

G-20 Capital Adequacy Frameworks Panel. *Boosting MDBs' Investing Capacity: An Independent Review of Multilateral Development Banks' Capital Adequacy Frameworks*. 2022.

International Monetary Fund. *Kenya – Fourth Reviews under the Extended Arrangement under the Extended Fund Facility and under the Arrangement under the Extended Credit Facility, and Requests for Augmentation of Access under the Arrangement under the Extended Credit Facility, and Modifications of Quantitative Performance Criteria.* IMF Country Report No. 22/382, December 2022.

International Monetary Fund. *Regional Economic Outlook, Sub-Saharan Africa: Light on the Horizon?* 2023.

International Monetary Fund. *Kenya 2023 Article IV Consultation*. IMF Country Report No. 24/13, 2024.

Jain, G., L. Palacios, and H. Verhoeven. *Can Debt-for-Climate Swaps Help Heavily Indebted Developing Countries Address Climate Priorities?* Center on Global Energy Policy at Columbia, 2023.

Index

Note: Page numbers in **bold** refer to tables, and those in *italics* refer to figures.